Presented To:

_____

From:

_____

Date:

_____

IGNITING

furious

LOVE

IGNITING

furious

LOVE

MATTHEUS VAN DER STEEN

HEIDI BAKER

GREG BOYD

ROLAND BAKER

PHILIP MANTOFA

SHAMPA RICE

WILL HART

ROBBY DAWKINS

ANGELA GREENIG

DESTINY IMAGE® PUBLISHERS, INC.
P.O. Box 310, Shippensburg, PA 17257-0310

"Promoting Inspired Lives."

This book and all other Destiny Image, Revival Press, MercyPlace, Fresh Bread, Destiny Image Fiction, and Treasure House books are available at Christian bookstores and distributors worldwide.

For a U.S. bookstore nearest you, call 1-800-722-6774.
For more information on foreign distributors, call 717-532-3040.
Reach us on the Internet: www.destinyimage.com.

ISBN 13 TP: 978-0-7684-4069-0
ISBN 13 Ebook: 978-0-7864-8901-9

For Worldwide Distribution, Printed in the U.S.A.

1 2 3 4 5 6 7 / 16 15 14 13 12

TABLE OF CONTENTS

INTRODUCTION

I honestly have no idea when I first dreamed up the Furious Love Event. There was no angelic encounter, no lightning bolt from Heaven, just a simple desire to fill what I perceived as a need within the Body of Christ for a wide variety of voices to come together in unity (even though they may not agree on everything) and bring teaching on some of the hot-button topics that my films have become known for. That was really the original idea, and thankfully, the end result not only met my expectations...it far exceeded them.

In my first book, *Filming God*, I detailed many of the crazy adventures I had around the world while making my first two films, *Finger of God* and *Furious Love*. These adventures and experiences, some of them almost too wild to be believed, eventually led this skeptical, cerebral kid full bloom into the belief in the active power of God in the world today. Many of the people I invited to speak at this event were the very ones who helped change my mind and shape my new theology—a theology, incidentally, that is 100 percent rooted in the Scriptures. The more I meet people and hear their stories, the more I realize that a lot of the popular theology bandied about these days (especially the stuff making God tame, normal, and fairly innocuous) is not lifted from the Bible, but more from people's experiences— or lack thereof. This was where I lived for quite a long time. I believed God could do stuff—shoot, I even saw Him move and do pretty cool stuff when I was a teenager going off to Bible camp—but those experiences were a long time ago, and I had grown up now. Sure He could move, do miracles, rock people's worlds, but I didn't see it happen very much anymore, so, you know, that's kind of where it ends.

I didn't believe God did much out in the open because I didn't see it happen on a regular basis. But then I started making this crazy film, *Finger of God*, and I began meeting people who DID see God moving on a regular basis. I went out with them as they attempted to embrace a desperate world and I began to see God move with my own eyes. And then it all started to click into place. God didn't do many miracles in my life (although He always worked behind the scenes on my behalf, because that's what He does with His kids, even the ones who aren't the most grateful or loving ones in His house) because I simply wasn't asking Him for any miracles. As I got to know these people— people like Heidi Baker, Will Hart, Robby Dawkins—I realized very quickly that they were not in possession of any special gift or proprietary spiritual secret; they were simply normal people with normal lives, normal concerns, normal marriages, just like me. But the one thing they did differently was not allow their fear to control them. When I saw need, I tried to ignore it because I was afraid of stepping out in faith. What was I afraid of? Failing. Making God look weak. Making myself look stupid. Should I keep going? I think you get the point.

Here's the thing: I have seen every single person you are about to encounter in this book fail. I have seen them pray for people and nothing happened. I have been with them when they stepped out so boldly and fell so flat that I was embarrassed for them. I have seen them all look stupid in the eyes of men. But never once did I ever look down on them for their effort. In reality, I felt ashamed for my own lack of effort.

One of my favorite things about God's Kingdom is the fact that His rules and how He looks at stuff is so wildly different from our rules and view of the world. For instance, for the most part we operate out of a success/failure mindset in just about every aspect of life. If you try to do something, you will either succeed or fail. The person you are praying for will either be healed or not. That altar call will produce results or not. Success or failure—those are our two options. It's true in business, sports, school, and especially in ministry. Fortunately for us, God does not operate out of a success/failure mindset. Never has. Just read the Bible, it's right there, plain as day. No, God operates out of a relationship/obedience model.

God cares so much more about our relationship with Him than He does what we can do for Him. If your "calling" is beginning to lead you away from His heart, He is not going to care how many people you are currently reaching—He will create circumstances that will either cause you to come back to His heart, to relationship, or He will shut down what you are doing. Even if it's for His Kingdom! Jesus tells us the Father is like the shepherd who leaves the 99 sheep to go find the one who has wandered off. I have to admit that I never understood this parable properly until I understood this basic truth. I always thought that was kind of silly of Him to possibly allow 99 sheep to now wander off while you go out and look for that one. The percentages didn't make sense. It seemed foolhardy. It wasn't the most fruitful use of His time and energy. But as hard as it is for us to comprehend, He cares more about you and your relationship with Him than He does what you can do for Him. This is the essence of love, isn't it?

Every one of the people you will encounter within these pages is doing amazing, massive things for the Kingdom of God. But every one of them realizes who they are in Christ as well. And that, more than their ministries or their wild stories, is why I have been drawn to them. They certainly aren't the only ones I have filmed with this foundation, not by a long shot, but they were chosen to be a part of this event simply because they represented the wonderfully divergent, multi-colored, and inclusive reality of the Kingdom of God. It was a thrill for me to sit with these men and women over dinner, for instance, and hear them talk with one another, debate theological points with one another (and to be honest, some of them believed the polar opposite of what others believed), but they were able to discuss things and relate to one another always in a spirit of love and unity. In our Father's house, we are free to disagree with each other, but we are never free to be unloving, and these nine wonderful people showed me the power of unity during the three days of the event.

You will read things in this book and watch things on our DVDs from the event, I'm sure, that will contradict or disagree with something someone else says. That's not a problem or something that should confuse you—it's kind of the point. There is room for many flavors and opinions in our Father's Kingdom. As long as we all agree on the major points—that Christ died for us, that our sins have been washed away and, therefore, we can now enjoy a wonderful relationship with the Creator of the Universe, and as long as we commit to loving the one in front of us, no matter what it costs us (money, dignity, pride, etc.), we can always agree to disagree.

My prayer is that this book and the DVDs we have created from this event will find and speak to you exactly where you are. Life and faith are, in essence, a journey. Wherever you are on this journey, be at peace and know that others are right there with you, and your Father is right behind you, cheering you on and happy beyond belief with who you are, right now, at this very moment.

—Darren Wilson
Director
Finger of God, Furious Love, Father of Lights

Chapter 1

IT'S ALL IN THE DELIVERY

by Mattheus van der Steen

I DIDN'T GROW UP IN very charismatic circles. My father was a Baptist pastor, and I grew up as a Baptist son. I don't have a big testimony like my wife has—rescued from satanism and drugs and all that stuff. I just don't have that. But when I was 14 years old, Jesus asked me, "Why are you going to church?" I really couldn't answer that question. I was going to answer the question, but the answer wasn't so nice, so I kept it to myself.

Then I went to my knees and the Lord overwhelmed me with His love. Afterward, I went to my father and said, "Daddy, I really gave my heart to the Lord, to Jesus." And he said, "Well, can we baptize you next week?" I said, "Yes." And I got baptized.

Even way back then, the Lord enjoyed sending me into funny situations. One day I said to my Baptist-pastor father, "Daddy, I'm reading my Bible, and I'm reading Acts, and it says that when you receive the Holy Spirit you will also speak in different tongues."

My father said, "Matt, you already speak in different languages. You're speaking French and German."

I said, "No, Daddy, that's not what I mean. There's like this additional power in the Bible, and I want to receive that power." Dad came to the conclusion that he couldn't give me an answer. But he said, "I have a very good friend and that friend has a brother who has a son…and he lives in England. So I'll fly you to England to meet him so you can figure out what you think you are missing."

I was never part of a charismatic movement. I didn't know anything about it. But there I was worshiping the Lord along with a band. Drums, at that time in my church, were from the devil. So I was in this tiny church and a big man—the pastor— came over to me. I was so afraid of him. He put his big hand on my head, and I was so nervous that my heart was beating out of my chest.

Before I knew it, I was down on the floor—I had never heard about this in my life. I was stuck on the floor for 20 minutes! I thought, *This is not nice.* And the big pastor looked over at me, smiled, and said, "How are you doing, cheese-head from Holland?" I'm like, *What? Cheese-head from Holland?* And the only thing I could say was "coolesheeky."

Well, I had never heard this word in my life, but he said, "You received the Holy Spirit, and you can speak in tongues now." So I went home very happy. My mom and dad picked me up from the airport, and asked, "Matt, do you speak in tongues?"

"Yes!" I said, "Coolesheeky!" My father said, "Wow, this is great!" And I was the talk of the town. Father tried and tried to speak in tongues, but nothing happened. One night while my mother was in the shower, I heard her singing, "Lord Jesus, fill me with your Holy Spirit." And suddenly she was speaking,

"Pizzeria, pizzeria. Pizzeria! And the next morning when I went to the kitchen for breakfast, Mom said, "Matt, I speak in tongues, too! Pizzeria!"

"Pizzeria!"

"Coolesheeky!"

Then again I was reading my Bible, and it says have faith like a child, and that signs and miracles will follow the believers, and we should lay hands on the sick. I was so excited! "Daddy, shall we have a healing service?"

He said, "Well, Matt, we may have a problem with this because our elder board has been discussing the color of the carpet for two years." I'll never forget that. Then he said, "Well, I'll ask the board, but when I do, I will probably get fired." In the end, he did get fired. But that's OK.

Because Mom and I spoke in tongues, Dad thought that we should follow through and have a healing service. So this is what we did. At that time we didn't have that much money to print flyers, so we wrote "Come to Jesus, receive your healing" on papers and handed them out. Two months later, we had the healing service. I woke up that day, and I felt very miserable. I can say that I didn't feel any anointing because I didn't know what anointing was. And so I said, "Daddy, I think we made a very big mistake," and we all prayed together that nobody would show up.

The time came and the band played—we had a drum in the church and people were angry, but it's OK if religious people get angry. Eighty people showed up, and to me it was like thousands of people were there. So my time came to preach, and I preached for about five minutes and then I said, "Please come forward if you want to receive healing." I was so nervous I kneeled down and I wondered if anybody would show up. Fifty people came forward.

On my left side was a boy, Robert, and I bowed toward him, and said, "Robert, please don't let it be serious," and then I realized that the tiny microphone had broadcast what I had said. Robert looked at me very shocked and said, "Well, Matt, I just returned from a missions trip and I have a parasite." That put me into a panic, because I didn't remember reading about parasites in the Word of God. And I had learned if it's not in the Word of God, it's not from the Lord. *Where's the parasite in your Word, Lord?* I didn't know what to do. Then I suddenly asked the Holy Spirit to help me.

I remembered an old tape that a relative asked me to watch of a healing service, so I said, "Come here, Robert." Following what I saw the healer do, I planted both feet firmly and then I tried to spit on him. The room was dead silent. I was shocked. Robert was shocked. I closed my eyes and I screamed, "In the name of Jesus, I rebuke this transvestite!" (Instead of parasite.)

That was my first healing meeting—17 years ago, maybe longer. I was 15 then. I was so afraid that the Lord was angry with me for my mistake. At that time, I didn't really know the Father heart of God. A few years later, I attended a church service in Canada and one of the leaders bowed over me and asked, "What was your biggest mistake?" Of course I mentioned what happened with Robert. He said, "Close your eyes and let me call to the Father." Suddenly I saw the Father in Heaven on His throne. Wow! And He said, "Matt, listen, do you remember that story?" I said, "Yeah, Daddy, it was so painful." He said, "No, it was the best joke ever." I couldn't believe His answer. What? I was so religious. Then I start laughing for hours and hours and since then I have been free to make these kinds of mistakes, knowing that He knows my heart and I know His.

I share these stories for a reason: don't be afraid to step out in faith. God still loves you if you make mistakes. He is proud of you for stepping out of the comfortable and into His special, handcrafted destiny for you.

See the Invisible, Do the Impossible

Paul said in Ephesians 3:20 that there is a power available beyond our thinking. I wanted to receive that power, the power that's even beyond our thinking. And the Lord said, "Close your eyes. When you see the invisible then I can do the impossible." I said, "Lord, I see ten nations, closed nations," and suddenly I saw Burma. "Lord, I want to go to Burma. I want to go to Pakistan."

I didn't have money, nothing to make me think I was ready to go, but two years ago one of the ten nations started to open up, Burma, or Myanmar, as it's known today. While I was preaching with a good friend of mine in Jakarta, at a conference of 1,500 ministry leaders, one of the pastors came up to me, told me his name, and said he came from Myanmar. "Can you please come to my nation?" he asked.

"Don't expect someone with a lot of clout," I said.

"No, I come only for you," he said.

And so we went to Myanmar. Unbelievable! God is so faithful.

I was a little bit nervous about traveling because one of the pastors in Holland called me while I was in the Amsterdam airport and said, "Matt, it's a very closed nation—you can't even take your cell phone with you."

Oh my gosh! This is not good. My iPhone 4 is my second wife; Rebecca's my first wife, of course. But I must obey the will of God. No nonsense. And so the Lord said, "Go for Me," and I went on to Myanmar. At that point, I didn't have a clue what to do next. I had brought four people with me, so there was no turning back. When we were close to landing in Myanmar, I said, "Lord, I just can't leave my iPhone behind. It's not possible. You need to give me a solution, please."

Well, I'll spare you the gory details about where in my body I concealed it, but suffice it to say that I had use of my iPhone while in Myanmar. When the pastor arrived to pick me up, he said, "Come, we go to the blind institute for a secret meeting." I thought about five people would show up because he only had a bicycle to spread the word, and there is little to no reliable mass communication services in the country. Amazingly, about 600 pastors showed up from across the nation.

We worshiped for three days and the Holy Spirit was with us. Two of the pastors had a dream to have a public, government-approved crusade in the Capitol city. Because the Bible says that when two or three agree in God's name, He will give it—we believed. We rented a taxi and went to the government building to seek permission. But we didn't even get permission to go in the building because the area was thick with police.

We then went to a small village and starting praying for the sick. A little girl, about six years of age, came to us. She was crippled and couldn't speak or hear. All we said was the name of Jesus and she received a complete healing. The story reached one of the generals in the government, and to make a very long story short, we got permission from the government, with protection from the army, to hold the very first public, government-sanctioned, government-sponsored crusade in a government building!

As excited as I was about the approval, I also felt worried. The building could fit more than 3,000 people—but what if the government was planning to come and kill all the pastors and people who come to the crusade. Christians were commonly killed in that country, which is 95 percent Buddhist. I had to have faith that God would protect us. People of the government came, the secret police came, people from across the country came, and they all bowed their knees to Jesus. After the four-day crusade, the government asked us to please come back, saying, "We will give you the biggest stadium in the city." Tens of thousands of Burmese people publicly worshiping the Lord is a miracle. Signs and miracles—this is God. We are living in a time when *everything is possible.*

Promises Fulfilled

The Word of God is full of the Lord's promises. But what I see happening in the Body of Christ is that people, who ask for the promises and don't see the fulfillment right away, are getting very disappointed.

In the following pages, I will give you the key to allowing God to fulfill your promise.

In Genesis, God gave Abraham promises. I can imagine God the Father, saying, "Hey, listen, Abraham, I'm going to make you a father of the nations." Even though that's a promise from the Lord, we know that Sarah, his wife, was laughing. At the age of 90, how could they have a child? Genesis 17:5 gives us insight: *"No longer will you be called Abram; your name will be Abraham, for I have made you a father of many nations."* God was saying, *I will make you a father for the nations. I will bless you. Kings will come to you. I will make you fruitful.*

But it took time between hearing the promise and seeing the promise fulfilled. And then after God fulfilled the promise, and Isaac was born, God tested Abraham.

> *He said to him, "Abraham!" "Here I am," he replied. Then God said, "Take your son, your only son, whom you love— Isaac—and go to the region of Moriah. Sacrifice him there as a burnt offering on a mountain I will show you"* (Genesis 22:1-2).

I believe that God wants to test us. I believe that Abraham was so in love with the Father and trusted Him so much that he was willing to do whatever the Father asked him to do. When God told Abraham to leave everything behind and go to the Promised Land, Abraham obeyed God without thinking. We can learn so much from Abraham. He and Sarah waited so long for God's promise to become a reality. They trusted Him. When Isaac arrived, they knew God's promise was fulfilled. They rejoiced! And then God asked the unimaginable, but Abraham obeyed.

Abraham's relationship with God overrode the sacrifice Abraham felt in offering his only son to God. Abraham was willing to pay the price to obey God. Abraham's sacrifice of Isaac meant sacrificing himself. God anointed Abraham with a promise, and Abraham had total faith in that promise. The anointing of the Lord is not only for you. The anointing from the Lord is for the nations, for the world, a dying world. Many people in the Body of Christ want to see the miracles, the signs, the revival, and the transformation, but they have not yet paid the price.

But you may be thinking, *Yeah, but Jesus paid the price on the cross.* I say to you, "Yes, but when Jesus died, there were two other crosses." There's a cross for you. If you are not willing to pick up that cross, you cannot be a disciple of Jesus Christ (see

Luke 9:23). This is furious love! Are you willing to sacrifice your life for Him? For the Gospel of Jesus Christ? Not out of law but out of love and compassion. God tested Abraham, and sometimes in life God will test you.

Abraham took the wood for the burnt offering and placed it on the altar. God the Father took the wood and placed it on the cross, and He Himself carried the fire and the knife. Can you imagine how emotional this process was for these two fathers who loved their only sons? No, we really can't, can we?

Allow me to paraphrase this story from Genesis 22:1-18: And as the two of them went together, Isaac said to his father, Abraham, "Father?" "Yes, my son." "The fire and the wood are here, but where is the lamb for the burnt offering?" Abraham said, "God Himself will provide the lamb for the burnt offering, my son." And the two of them went on together and when they reached the place God told him about, Abraham built an altar there and arranged the wood, and he bound his son Isaac, and he laid him on the altar on top of the wood.

Abraham was willing to sacrifice the promise to obey God, even though he didn't know that this would be the fulfillment of the promise. Many people are waiting for the fulfillment of the promise and the only thing that has to happen is sacrifice. Sacrificing your life is not cheap.

Abraham built an altar, and then he reached out his hand and took the knife to slay his son. Praise the Lord for angels!

But the angel of the Lord called out to him from Heaven saying, "Abraham, Abraham!"

"Here I am," he replied.

"Do not lay a hand on the boy," he said. "Do not do anything to him. Now I know that you fear God because you have not withheld from me your son, your only son."

Abraham looked up and there in the thick he saw a ram caught by its horns. He went over and took the ram and sacrificed it as a burnt offering instead of his son. Abraham called that place the Lord will provide. And the angel of the Lord called to Abraham from Heaven a second time and said "I swear by myself, declares the Lord, that because you have done this and have not withheld your son, your only son, I will surely bless you and make your descendants as numerous as the stars in the sky and as the sand on the seashore. Your descendants will take possession of the cities of the enemies, and through your offspring all nations on earth will be blessed because you have obeyed Me" (Genesis 22:11-18).

Believers need to do something very radical—we need to embrace the cross. And I'm not referring to the cross of Jesus, because that cross is empty. Do you know what the cross means? The cross is the end of you. Jesus Christ died on the cross so that you could live in Him. You have to die on your cross so that Jesus can live in you. That is worth repeating: *Jesus Christ died on the cross so that you could live in Him. You have to die on your cross so that Jesus can live in you.*

God's Very Big Dream

In Genesis 37 Joseph received a dream. And he shared that dream with his brothers, and I'm sure you remember what happened. Instead of brothers saying, "Yes, fantastic!" there was jealousy. There was envy! When God gives you a very big dream, it is very likely that the closest people around you are not so happy with that dream. They feel a little bit uncomfortable. And it is also a possibility that some people who are very close to you will betray you.

And you can do two things with betrayal—you can become bitter or better. And sometimes it is important to remember that betrayal can actually launch you into your destiny. That's another secret. If you haven't died to yourself and you get betrayed, it hurts you so much that your reaction says more about you than the betrayal. It is a fact that when you want to operate in signs and miracles and in the promises and spiritual things of the Lord, you will be attacked and persecuted. And if you are not dead to yourself, if you haven't given yourself totally over to Jesus, attacks and betrayals hurt so much that you draw back. You lose your confidence.

Throughout Hebrews we are told not to lose our confidence—to be confident in the Lord and ourselves. For instance, Hebrews 10:35 says, *"So do not throw away your confidence; it will be richly rewarded."* When you don't die to yourself, you get disappointed, offended by people, and don't see the fulfillment of your promise, you shrink back (see Heb. 10:38). When you lose your confidence, in the end you can lose the crown of glory on your life—the anointing.

And so Joseph had a dream. Don't wait for the favor of others. If you have a dream, follow it. Be obedient to the dream God has given to you. When Joseph's brothers saw that their father loved him more than any of them, they hated Joseph and could not speak a kind word to him. Then they hated him all the more because of his dream and the idea that the nations would be bowing to him. In Israeli culture, the oldest son Judah should have received the honor. But in this case, Joseph received the honor and actually received the most beautiful mantle—and his brothers envied him. They were very jealous. So Judah and his brothers sold Joseph for their own sake.

Joseph's brothers sold him for 20 silver shillings. Every brother received two shillings, and I believe that those two coins became very heavy in Judah's life. Very heavy. Then came a devastating famine in the land. Through many twist and turns, Joseph's life went through a whole series of transformations, and he became a very high government official. In Genesis 43, Scripture tells us that the brothers went back to Egypt and took their youngest brother Benjamin along as Joseph had requested. Deeply moved at the sight of his brother, Joseph hurried out and looked for a place to weep and he went into his private room and he wept there.

What happened next? Joseph gave his brothers grain and silver to take home. He instructed one of his servants to put a special, silver cup into Benjamin's grain sack and sent his brothers home. Then Joseph sent a servant after them to accuse them of acting dishonestly and stealing his silver cup. When the cup was discovered in Benjamin's sack, Joseph dismissed the brothers and declared that Benjamin would become a slave for his crime. Judah spoke up, however, and said, *"Now then, please let your servant [me] remain here as my lord's slave in place of the boy, and let the boy return with his brothers. How can I go back to my father if the boy is not with me? No! Do not let me see the misery that would come on my father"* (Genesis 44:33-34). This is Judah's transformation. Judah didn't live for his own sake anymore. He was willing to sacrifice his life for the love of his father and for the boy.

In many ministries and churches, it is evident that people are not living for others; they live for themselves and they sell their people for a few coins. Some abuse their people to accomplish their own visions and dreams. And God is crying. It hurts His heart. Do we live life for our own sakes, for our own pleasure, or are we willing to die, to take up our crosses and live for

Jesus and to live for a dying world instead of living for our own little selfish lives?

Your Cross

When I think about revival, I don't think about a church full of people. I think about people full of God. If you are willing to sacrifice your life to Jesus, you will experience a deeper level of commitment to the Lord. That means you give everything to Him. Everything. Luke 9:23 says, *"Then He [Jesus] said to them all: 'Whoever wants to be My disciple must deny themselves and take up their cross daily and follow Me."* Dear friend, this is furious love. Nobody's willing to take up their cross without that incredible furious love that the Holy Spirit wants to give us to strengthen us. Jesus said, *"And whoever does not carry their cross and follow Me,"* this isn't referring to the cross of Jesus, it's about *your* cross in your life, *"cannot be My disciple"* (Luke 14:27).

I'm not talking about being saved or being a Christian. This is about being a disciple. I hear people who say, "I want to follow Jesus, whatever the cost." On hearing Jesus' command to follow Him, *"many of His disciples said, 'This is a hard teaching. Who can accept it?'"* (John 6:60). Then many of His disciples turned back and no longer followed Him. I pray that the Holy Spirit will fill you up with strength and peace. We need to preach the cross again and teach about the sacrifice that disciples of Christ must make.

> Father, You gave Your only Son, Jesus, on the cross. And Lord, we're so sorry we took You for granted. Help us, Lord, to fix our eyes on You and not on our little world. Lord, we want to be part of Your dream. That's a world being saved, full of Your glory; but Lord, a fulfillment

of the promises You gave to us will only be fulfilled by sacrifice.

Although Joseph was betrayed by his brothers, accused wrongly, and was imprisoned, he remembered God's promise. Although you may have been betrayed, wrongly accused, and imprisoned, you must remember God's promise to you. Having faith in His faithfulness will get you through every challenge in life.

Many people feel like they are being thrown away like Joseph was sold. I pray that we, as God's Church, will stop feeding ourselves, and that we will start seeing the dying world for which Jesus died. Let's write a covenant with the Lord so He can fill in His promises and we can obey Him. Let's sacrifice our lives and choose to live for God and the world around us—for His glory.

More Than We Can Ask or Imagine

Now I want to explain something about the anointing and the Great Commission and how they are connected. Ephesians 3:20, one of my favorite Scriptures, says, *"Now to Him who is able to do immeasurably more than all we ask or imagine, according to His power that is at work within us."* I love the bottom-line message—God can do anything.

My wife knows me the best, besides Jesus, and she would say that I'm the most ordinary, simple man ever. There's nothing special about me. Jesus and my wife know me and where I came from. They know that I am not able on my own to stand up in front of thousands of people worldwide and preach—this is possible only with the power available through God. I use up His love and power to spread His Word. When I try on my own, many times I have a big mouth but a very small heart. Many times I'm the little boy giving his lunch to Jesus so He can multiply it. You may feel like that too sometimes.

There is a power available beyond even what you are thinking, praying, and dreaming right now, and the power is available today. And even though it will cost you everything, your sacrifice will bring not only signs and miracles, it will bring the Kingdom of God right into your spirit, home, community, church, and nation. What is invisible in Heaven is visible on earth.

This power has nothing to do how much you pray or fast; it's a power that you receive through a sacrificial life. That's the key; and the enemy is very busy talking to our minds, talking us out of receiving the power we need to defeat him. My wife, Rebecca, came out of the occult and she knows about spiritual warfare. She knows. She's a seer. She sees angels, demons, and all that stuff. I only see her, my beautiful wife.

We came to the conclusion a few years ago that the biggest battles are not between angels and demons or between you and satan—they are the battles going on in your head. The biggest spiritual warfare happens within your mind, in your thinking. The power of God renews your mind and suddenly you start seeing that there is a power available for your use that is beyond your wildest dreams. This power breaks the chains of your finite thinking.

We have to realize it is not only who we are in Christ. God is also saying I created you and you are the crown of My creation. I made you in My image. In other words, God made us like Him. Jesus even said that we will do even greater things that He did! (See John 14:12.)

Everything that happened in the New Testament can happen today—including the multiplication of food. That power is available for you today, now; and satan hates it. When you realize that the power is available for you, I almost want to beg you to stop praying for your vision and stop praying for the will of God in your life. Why? God's will for your life is for you to come alive. The will of God is that you start doing what's in the Bible. Go and preach the Gospel—share the Good News with others. The will of God for you is to take care of orphans and widows. The will of God is for you to love yourself and your neighbor and God as much as possible. Stop praying for the will of God in your life and start doing the stuff Jesus told you to do. Don't walk away from your responsibility.

In my beginning Christian years, I struggled a lot. I was so afraid of not doing God's will. I was so afraid that it made me passive. We have to break the chain of passivity and walk in the freedom of the Holy Spirit to do what's in our hearts to do. God can do anything—far more than we could ever imagine or guess or request in our wildest dreams. He does it not by pushing us around but by working His spirit deeply and gently within us. That's what the Lord is going to do with us again and again—our lives will be changed when we finally realize that everything is possible.

Too Focused on Manifestations

If we are too focused on the manifestations, we miss our goal. Let me share a very honest example with you. In 2011, we held a revival meeting in my nation of Holland, and usually many manifestations occurred during meetings—people rolling all over the floor, laughter, and the like. But this time nothing seemed to happen. In fact, one lady came to me very upset. She said, "I didn't feel God tonight. He was not here. His presence was not here."

I wanted to rebuke her like Jesus said to Peter, "You, satan, get behind her," but I couldn't say that. Then I thought, *What if Abraham would have only gone by manifestation feelings, he may have never followed through with taking Isaac to the altar.* Today, in a lot of charismatic movements, manifestations have become so important that if there are none, people conclude God's presence must not be there. What nonsense! God is always with us. Always. We have to be careful that we don't say, "Oh, He's not here," if we don't feel God's presence.

There must be a balance between our feelings, feeling God, and walking in faith. Many times your feelings lie to you. Don't fall into the trap. You will be embarrassed. Don't go by your feelings only; go by faith. God is going to release faith in your spirit and heart.

Someone came to me and said, "I have a dream." I said, "Try to put your dream on paper. Then find two or three people who believe in you and start agreeing together for that dream. Maybe it will end up looking different from the original, but God will do something when two or three people are agreeing about something." I challenge you to do the same. Start writing things down on paper. Start gathering around people who believe in you, who are not envious and jealous of you, but who believe in you. Most ministry leaders can help you, but if you cannot find leaders, find children.

Focus on Jesus

If you want to walk in revival and transformation, you cannot do it yourself. Jesus must be our focus. He was making this point to Philip and Andrew when the multitude was hungry. The disciples wanted to send the people away. But Jesus told them to feed the people (see Matt. 14:16). So there were about

20,000 people who needed to be fed. The disciples looked at each other and then found a young boy with two fish and five loaves of bread. Then they focused on Jesus again and explained the situation. That's faith—always seeking the solution to every problem by focusing on Jesus.

Do you look up when Jesus brings you into a situation that you don't know how to handle? Are you looking to God? Are you looking to Jesus? Or are you looking at the circumstances and saying, "There's no way I can pay that bill this month"? I know what I'm talking about. We have taken care of more than 900 kids all over the world. We had stressful moments and every moment we had to choose. But because we have Jesus, we go on our knees, and we commit everything to Him. We say, "Lord, here it is." And believe it or not, every month our bills have been paid and sometimes we have months of overflow. Jesus is our Provider.

So fix your eyes on Jesus, and when reality hits, you will pass the test. Remember, though, God is not angry when you don't pass the test. Maybe He has to tell satan to get behind us, but that's OK as long as we learn to pass the test. I still fail sometimes. When we fix our eyes on Jesus and go from breakthrough to breakthrough and start believing what the Word of God says, suddenly the battles in our minds are broken, we know that everything is possible, and the anointing flows.

• • •

Thank You, Lord, that You gave us the most incredible power and the most powerful weapon in this world—Your anointing paid with the blood of Jesus—because, Lord, You had to go to the Father to release Your anointing upon Your people. And Lord, we are proud that our last name is Christian. Lord, we are proud that Your last name is Christ, the anointed One. Thank You, Lord, that You anointed us to finish what You started on this earth, because we realize, Father, we are entering into a time when You are coming back soon. Where darkness covers the earth, Your glory will arise upon Your people.

I thank You, Lord, that You are going to release that anointing on us for the world, for the nations. We don't have a clue where to go or how to do it, but Lord, it's all about You. Right now, we just want to receive Your anointing and connect that with the Great Commission. We want to receive that anointing not for ourselves but so we can deliver it to the dying world around us, for the brokenness all around. I pray, Lord, that we use the power of God and that faith will be released in our hearts. May faith, love, and confidence be released in our inner beings—thank You, Jesus.

Chapter 2

CALLED TO FEED THE HUNGRY

by Heidi Baker

So HERE's A GREAT STORY. It's from the Book of Luke 14:12, *"Then Jesus said to his host, 'When you give a luncheon or dinner...'"* (emphasis added). What? What did He say? What was the word? You got it—*when*. Jesus didn't say *if*. He didn't say *if* you feed the poor. He didn't say *if* you give a luncheon or a dinner.

My husband, Rolland, and I have over 10,000 kids in our care in our ministry in Mozambique; and believe me, they all like to eat every day. Fasting is mandatory on Mondays and they hate it, but it's for God. We are called to eat. We need to eat what's good; eat Jesus, drink Jesus, be filled with Jesus all the time (see Matt. 26:26-28). So, *"When you give a luncheon or a dinner, do not invite your friends, your brothers or sisters, your relatives, or your rich neighbors; if you do, they may invite you back and so you will be repaid"* (Luke 14:12).

But when you give a banquet, invite the poor, the crippled, the lame, the blind, and you will be blessed. Although they cannot repay you, you will be repaid at the resurrection of the righteous. When one of those at the table with Him heard this, he said to Jesus, "Blessed is the one who will eat at the feast in the Kingdom of God" (Luke 14:13-15).

Have you heard some offerings lately? "But when you give a banquet, invite the poor." What? What did He say? "Invite the poor, the crippled, the lame, the blind." When you give a party or a feast, Jesus says to invite the poor and those who are disabled.

Maybe you are poor, crippled, blind, and lame. You may be spiritually crippled. Maybe you feel like you can't run because you need to be ignited by the power of God and you don't feel like a runner, you don't feel full of God—you're the one God invited to a feast today. If you're invited to His feast—and you are—then you must eat and drink because there's something about hunger that delights the heart of God, and there's something about a lack of hunger that makes Him very, very sad. Are you hungry? He's so delicious.

Jesus took bread, and when He had given thanks, He broke it and gave it to His disciples, saying, "Take and eat; this is my body." Then He took a cup, and when He had given thanks, He gave it to them, saying, "Drink from it, all of you. This is My blood of the covenant, which is poured out for many for the forgiveness of sins" (Matthew 26:26-28).

Remember, when you invite to your table the poor and the disabled, you will be blessed, for, *"Although they cannot repay you, you will be repaid in the resurrection of the righteous"* (Luke 14:14).

We like to eat and we like to feed people. Every day we're feeding people—sometimes as many as 100,000 people. The number depends on whether it's flood or famine time in the country. When our daughter got married, we were happy for the opportunity to feed people. First we had a small reception in the United States with about 200 people, and then we had the real one in Mozambique with about 4,000 people! I remember the day well because we bought every chicken in all of Cabo Delgado, every live chicken. We killed them and cooked them; and we bought all of the eggs to make cakes. All of the children made cakes, and all the staff made cakes, and all the missionaries made cakes, everybody was making cakes—hundreds and hundreds of cakes. It was so exciting for everyone.

Then we made invitations and gave them out to everyone we could find. The villagers had never received a real invitation to a feast of any kind. We also invited the blind and told them to bring along their guides. We invited the crippled and some came crawling in the dirt. We invited the poorest of the poor and some came in rags. We had this beautiful feast laid out and they all sat in the front. It was so glorious!

The cake time was a crazy scene. Because no one from the villages had ever tasted cake, except the children who live with us, hundreds of little children were quickly reaching, reaching for the pieces of cake. It was amazing to watch the joy of the Lord on the faces of those kids eating cake. That's the kind of party I like to have—watching the Kingdom of God break in over all those who accepted the invitation.

Miss Magdalene

Not long ago, I was in church and it was hot—probably 100-105 degrees. Afterward, a lady came up to me carrying a small child; I could tell she was very old and very, very poor. She was in rags, and she had tattoos all over her face. She handed me the little girl who had a big bloated belly and tiny little arms the size of my finger. She was limp and had no strength in her body; her little head drooped down and her legs didn't move. The woman handed me this little girl who was starving to death and said, "This is Miss Magdalene, will you take her?" She told me that the child's mom and dad died and she was the great aunt, "I have nothing. I have nothing at all. Please take her." I started to cry, "Jesus, You brought us another treasure…You brought us another treasure, Jesus."

Then I felt the joy of the Lord, and I watched as our beautiful brothers and sisters fed her. I was so happy that we could help her. She was so beautiful. I knew God was going to save her, and after about four days of being fed, she could lift up her little head. Even though she was three years old she couldn't even lift her head because she was so weak from starvation. But after four days, she could lift up her head and look at us.

The Lord said to me, "So much of My Church is dying of starvation and they're just like Magdalena. They don't even know how to eat. When you feed them, they vomit it out because they don't know how to eat—their digestion doesn't know what it is to eat real food." He said, "My Church needs to learn to eat. They need to learn to eat what's good. They need to drink what's good," He said. "And when they understand and they start to partake of My goodness, their heads will lift up and their legs will become strong and they will be able to run the race."

Thank You, Jesus!

You are called to run the race. You're called to live in the light of His glory and love. You're not called to be little, wimpy, starving-to-death orphans. You're called to be full of the Kingdom glory of God.

Blessed Is the One

When I saw this little girl begin to get strength, I was seeing a miracle. She gobbled down little packets of sugar. She grew stronger and now she's full of the glory of God in just a few months. She smiles and engages with people around her. If you, beloved of God who are starving and dying from lack of nourishment, from lack of pure food from the Gospel, if you eat and drink of Jesus, you will become strong, too. You will see what He sees, hear what He hears, and you will go where He goes. He is a glorious Savior who wants to feed you. He wants to feed you Himself.

> *When one of those at the table with Him heard this, he said to Jesus, "Blessed is the one who will eat at the feast in the Kingdom of God"* (Luke 14:15).

I remember this story in Luke because I always think of Christians who want to eat pie in the sky when they die. Many think, *God, we'll hold on. Jesus, we'll make it in our little living room. We'll hold on and keep our kids safe and we'll keep them away from all the darkness. We'll just hold on right here, and then we'll die, and then we'll all be happy in Heaven.*

There's actually more to life than that. You're called to carry the glory of God. You're called to be a carrier of the glory, carrier of the love, carrier of the power of God. You're not called to just hold on until you die one day and eat pie forever. Seriously, that is not going to do it for you. You're called to carry the feast, the love, the glory, the Kingdom of God out to the darkness. That's what you're called to do.

And sometimes you're called to allow people to see the darkness, because they don't even know how to bring the food or where to go. We have to see in order to understand, and God wants to give us eye salves so we can see what He sees and do what He does. Complacency in the Church has made us weak-limbed and weak-hearted. It's time to get hungry again. It's time to get strong. You need to eat and drink what's good. Stop living on cotton candy and diet cola. It is not nourishing you. Self-help? He wants to help you, but He wants to help you in a way that's holy and pure. He wants to give you an ability to see and strength to go.

I see in the Church in the Western world that so many are dying of starvation, spiritually dying of starvation and mal-nourishment because they are eating things that do not bring nourishment. God wants to give His Church what's real. Too many are just trying to hold on.

Do you know that there is a world desperate for Jesus? I minister worldwide and I see desperate people everywhere—even when I spoke at Harvard and MIT. There's no place where people aren't desperate for Jesus—if you show them the real Jesus. Carry what's good and real. If you feed them what is not food, they'll vomit it. We need to carry what's pure, holy, and Kingdom-based.

*"And Jesus replied, 'A certain man was preparing a great banquet and invited **many** guests'"* (Luke 14:16). *Many*, he invited many, many guests. Daddy God invites the entire world. He invites every broken, dying, desperate person in the entire world to His feast, but the only way they know is when someone tells them.

Called to Shine

Even though I speak at conferences a third of my life, two-thirds of my life is going to find the lost and the broken. I sit in mud huts to share Jesus with the most unnoticed people on the planet. My heart burns for the lost. My heart burns for the broken, and I felt the same way when I got to Harvard as I do when I'm walking on dirt roads. I feel the same kind of desperation in my heart; these people are dying, these people are hungry, these people are in need—and I say, "God, send me. Here I am, send me, Lord."

But I don't just want to be sent. I'm contending for an army of laid-down lovers who will give themselves for love. Will it be you? You're called to be a laid-down lover. You're called to carry the beauty of Jesus to the dark places. You're called to carry the glory of God. Why are you thinking about just holding on when God has called you to shine. God has called His children to shine light into the dark places of the world, your community, school, and family.

When Jesus said "a certain man," we know He's talking about Father God. Father God is the one preparing a massive banquet. There were many guests invited and when the preparations had been finished, He sent out His servant to tell those who had been invited, "Come, for everything is now ready." We are His servants. We need to tell all people everywhere that the banquet is set and they are invited to sit and eat with their Savior.

It is as simple as that. Will you invite them?

I get to see what you maybe don't see. I see the actual dying woman, the starving little boys and girls, the broken men, the dirty little orphans, the actual heartbroken widows. I see them. I hold them. I feed them; but it's not just me. It's now thousands of us together. That is my great privilege.

But for you, you often cannot see them because your eyes have gotten dimmed. Somehow you think if somebody drives a Lexus and goes to a banquet hall for a five-star meal that they're not dying of starvation. But beloved of God, if they don't know Jesus, they're dying.

We must not be ashamed of the Gospel. I'm not ashamed of the Gospel. I'm willing to die for Jesus, and I put myself in those places many times. I've been shot at, beat up, thrown in jail, slammed against walls, and had knives held to my throat so many times, but it's a fearless love and that for me is a privilege—being stoned is a privilege.

But where I find it most difficult is stepping into the Western world where people who were invited to the banquet feast show up and think, *Hmm, I wonder what's on the menu? I wonder if I want anything on the menu. I wonder if it's going to taste good enough for me.* That's when I have a bit of trouble because I see how God feels about hunger and how He feels about a lack thereof. I believe He wants to cause a holy hunger to rise up inside of you, a hunger for the beauty of who He is, a hunger for true food, a hunger for the true bread of Jesus. But not just a hunger for you, but a delight in your heart to give away what is real to a dying world. They really need to eat. They really need to drink.

I remember seeing the banqueting feast years ago in a vision. It was a beautiful vision. It was full color. The vision was of an incredible feast laid out on a table. I've seen the feast two times in very clear visions. One time when I saw the feast, I was in the garbage dump with Jesus and we were calling people to eat and they were being healed. When the Lord called them, I got to go with Him and call them home—they all went to the front at the wedding feast. The Lord said, "You sit in front those of you who are hungry." Since that day, I started to work in the garbage dump, finding people who lived there, until they put a wall around it. Then I moved to the north and we have a powerful work there—in the garbage dump area, it's powerful. Hundreds and hundreds of people have come to know Jesus.

Another time I saw the wedding feast table in front of me and it was as far as I could see to the left and as far as I could see to the right. On it was an amazing arrangement of every kind of food imaginable—incredibly beautiful, fresh food. And I saw Father God, not in His full glory, but I saw Father God and the image of Him sitting at the table. The seats behind Him and to the right and the left were empty. And then I saw little church people, Christians, and they ran in front of the table like little mice. They'd pick up a little piece of food off the table and run off, almost like they were stealing it. They couldn't understand that they were called to sit next to the Father. They were called to eat at the table, but instead they were eating little bits of food and scurrying off.

And then I saw Father look one in the eye and say, "You, come and sit with Me. You're My favorite." And then He did it again. "You're my favorite, come sit with me." I thought, *God, You told two of them that both were Your favorite. My theology kicked in, Oh, of course, He's omnipotent, omnipresent. Hey, we can all be His favorite. Yeah, Daddy's favorite and I can sit right next to Him and eat and drink with My Daddy God, and I can eat as much as I like. I could be as full of the Holy Spirit as I like. I want to be fuller still.*

Do you know what my prayer is every day, every single day? I wake up and I say, "Possess me Holy Spirit, every day." Every day for 36 years I've been praying, possess me Holy Spirit. Every day I say, "God, I want to know what it looks like to be fully possessed. I want to know what it looks like to be fully possessed by You, Holy Spirit. If You ever, ever want a volunteer on the earth, Lord, hey, let it be me."

Do you want to sign up for that? It means your life is not your own. There is a dying to self, which could upset your Western-world theology. There really is a saying that goes, "God, not my will but Yours be done; and I know that when I get close enough to You, my will and Your will become the same." So it's both and more but until you get to that place, until you get to that fully yielded place, it's always, always more of Him until when He lays down, you lay down and when He stands up, you stand up—He is living through you. You can have as much of the Holy Spirit as you want, but God is looking for those who will yield, who will open their hearts and their spirits to the power and presence of the Most High God.

Stop Snoring, Wake Up

There's a feast. It's ready, and so many are hungry, and so many haven't even heard, and so many aren't interested. I don't want to pick on the Western Church—I love the Western Church, but it's time to wake up. Do you know that every week in Africa I am privileged to lead hundreds, sometimes thousands, of people to Jesus? Do you know that almost no one ever says no to the Gospel there? Can you just imagine for a second what it would mean, what it would cost, for thousands of people in the Western nations to come to Jesus? I pray that you will catch His fire and that you will go—go to your family and friends, your schools, your colleges, your malls, your neighborhoods, and beyond. I'm here to call you to go, and to urge you to see what He sees and do what He does.

Another time I had a powerful vision. I heard the Lord, and when He spoke to me it was like a thundering, booming sound. He said, "Tell the Church to wake up, wake up, wake up sleeping beauty." I saw especially the Western Church snoring, and I saw the Lord, "Come, wake up, wake up, tell them to wake up, the feast is ready and they're asleep!" Then I saw Jesus kiss the Church and wake it with a kiss. Intimacy unto fruitfulness.

He's not going to shake you out of your sleep, He's going to kiss you; He wants to wake you up, beautiful bride. He wants to wake you up and calls you to shine for the light of His glorious love. He wants to send you across the street and around the world. He wants to send you as a lover to bring home the poor, crippled, blind, lame, lost, dying, and the sick.

Years ago I had such a small vision. Prophets would tell me that my vision was too small. One day the Lord spoke to me very clearly and said, "You're going to bring home 10,000 orphans." My response? "Yes, God." And we started bringing them home; eventually we welcomed more than 10,000 orphans. Even before we had 10,000 orphans, the Lord gave me another vision: He said, "You're called to bring home a million orphans."

My response? "Whoa, God, do You understand the logistics of that? You know we already have hundreds of trucks, but a million orphans? That's like tens of thousands of trucks, God, do You understand what that's going to take?" As if He doesn't know, I was trying to explain to God the logistics and how many buildings and how many planes, and trucks, and ships it would take. "God, do You know how much food it takes to feed that many children?" and He was just chuckling.

So not long afterward, I attended a conference. As I was worshiping God, kneeling and praising Jesus for the million children, prophets came and again told me that my vision was too small. They told me to believe God to bring home a million children in our movement. Something clicked in my brain and in my heart, and I realized that God wanted me to add to our ministry before I die. For years I had prayed to be martyred; absolutely, no questions, that's the only way to go. But now I have a vision of being martyred at age 120. Either I want to be taken up or martyred; both are good. But now I have such a desire to live for God, to see the vision fulfilled.

God spoke to me while I was snorkeling one day. He told me to build a university. I'm like, *Yeah, OK,* and swam away. Just recently, I was walking on this particularly large piece of land we bought in Cabo Delgado, Pemba, and I was looking around, walking through grass that was up to my waist—it's Africa. I was so happy because I started having visions from God about the university. I had the engineer behind me and the architect behind me, and I had another guy behind me who has already built a couple of universities. There were also a bunch of my kids behind me, and I told them all that they will get to attend this university. These are children that we picked up out of the dirt and the garbage—little girls who were bought and sold for a bottle of soda pop. They screamed with excitement when they heard they could go to the university. It was a very happy moment for all of us!

When God asks us if we want a nation, He doesn't just ask us and then expect us to just go sit on a rock. If God asks us if we want a nation, we're going to have to build things and do things and go places. God gives us visions, but some just sit on a rock. "Oh, let's watch the news. There's a new sitcom I want to see." Why do some just want to sit? They may not be sitting on a rock, but too many are sitting on a couch watching stuff that just doesn't matter. Weather report—brain fog.

When you see God's vision in your spirit, it will happen. Some don't see the food, don't see how real Jesus is and so they don't have a desperation to feed the poor and the dying—they just can't see it yet. Maybe they are ashamed of who He is and a little afraid to tell anybody that they're believers. But if they understood what they have, what they have been given, who He is, what He has given them to eat and drink, and how desperate the dying really are, then they would be motivated to eat more, and drink more, and feed the lost and the dying.

Excuses, Excuses

But they all alike began to make excuses. The first said, "I have just bought a field, and I must go and see it. Please excuse me." Another said, "I have just bought five yoke of oxen, and I'm on my way to try them out. Please excuse me." Still another said, "I just got married, so I can't come" (Luke 14:18-20).

Jesus told the servant lover to go and tell everyone that the feast was ready, so they went out and started talking to people. But everybody was making excuses: I'm too busy, busy, busy matching my towels and my sheets. I'm not able to come. Thank you for the invitation though; I'll take a rain check. I'm looking for a new car. It is extraordinarily important to me, and I'm going to make payments on it, and so it's going to take me some time to figure it all out so I'm really, really busy, and I'm going to have to have a rain check. I'm not able to come. I'm getting married. I'm having a wedding. I'm having a feast. I'm getting married so please, please, please just accept my apologies. I cannot come to the feast because I am having my own, thank you very much.

And the servant lover came back and reported this to the master and the owner of the house (see Luke 14:21). Who is the Master? God. Who owns the house? God. Daddy God, the Father of lights who holds everything in the palm of His hand and wants every lost son and daughter to come home. He is the Father of the feast, and He paid for the feast with His own Son's blood. He paid a spectacular price so that every son, every daughter, every broken and abandoned child on the planet— whether they be in the dumps of Mozambique, Harvard, or Oxford University—could be called to His Kingdom, to live in the glory love and to carry the presence.

Every man, woman, and child on God's green earth needs to eat and drink Jesus—or they die. Don't be ashamed of the feast. Don't be ashamed of what you have been given. Don't be ashamed of it. Hold on to what you have been given, so that every day, for the rest of your life, you can share what you have with the dying. Share your bread with the dying. Share your wine with the dying. Their dying may not look like your dying, but they are dying just the same. And if you see like Jesus and you see like the Father, you'll know they're dying, and you will want to help.

Father God gets angry when people are hungry but they don't eat. Jesus died to give us life—to fill us with Himself. When people make excuses and say they are not in need, they are fooling themselves—not God. Blessed are the poor in spirit for theirs is the Kingdom of Heaven. God wants to cause a holy hunger to rise up in you, a holy hunger not just for yourself but for your nation. God wants to cause you to be hungry for your nation.

> *The servant came back and reported this to his master. Then the owner of the house became angry and ordered his servant, "Go out quickly into the streets and alleys of the town and bring in the poor, the crippled, the blind and the lame"* (Luke 14:21).

The Master is telling us to go out quickly. You don't have to go to Sudan to go out quickly. It will take you three days to get to our base. The Congo is a really good place to go, but you might get killed faster than you expected. But just go out, just go. Go to 7/11, go out to Wal-Mart, go to Target, go to the grocery store. Surely you can find someone to feed every day.

"What if nobody is hungry?" you ask. If you get into the presence, into the intimate presence of God, if you get into the holy place, if you're connected with Jesus, in love with Jesus, breathing, eating, dreaming with Jesus—then fresh bread, the bread of presence is in your hands and even the rich cannot resist fresh, fresh bread.

You need fresh bread every day. You can eat it right now. The only place you get fresh bread is in His presence, and you can't wait until Sunday, you can't wait until Wednesday evening, you can't wait until a conference. *You need to get in the presence of God every day and receive the fresh bread from Heaven.* You can't wait to get fresh bread at some meeting. You need to learn how to live in the glory presence of God yourself, so that every day you never stop stopping for the Lord.

The servant came back and he said "We did it. We went out and brought the people in, but there is still room" (see Luke 14:22). Is there still room for more people in God's house? Yes! I'm a builder. I love to evangelize, and I love to build, so every week not only do I build things on bases but I'm always building houses—a couple of houses a week minimum just because I enjoy it and because there are a lot of homeless people. As I'm building, I'm thinking, *There are so many people who are still out there sleeping under trees. God, I want to see more houses built.* Then I have a vision of His Kingdom and I think, *There's room for everyone in Your Kingdom, no one is homeless in Your Kingdom. No one is starving in Your Kingdom. Lord, I want Your Kingdom to come on earth as it is in Heaven. So, Lord, let me carry Your Kingdom on earth as it is in Heaven. I want to see. I want to go. I want to do what You do. I want to see every homeless, dying, broken person in a home.* I'm a fanatic about it.

Did you ever meet a fanatic? I am one. I'm not afraid of it, and I don't mind if somebody says I'm a fanatic. Google it: fanatic. That's me. I'm a fanatic in the sense that I desperately want every child to come home, and I want to see God's Kingdom on earth.

Then the master told his servant, "Go out to the roads and country lanes and compel them to come in, so that my house will be full. I tell you, not one of those who were invited will get a taste of my banquet" (Luke 14:23).

Yikes.

• • •

Lord, we want to connect with You. Lord, we want to live in Your glory. We want to take our little lives and lay them at Your feet today. God, please take our lives and explode passion in us; explode compassion in us, Lord. I pray You rid us of all falsehood, Lord Jesus. Lord, let any double motives, double mindedness, and double initiatives go this day in Jesus' name. Lord, let the purity of Your love rise up in Your people. Let single-hearted devotion come to us, Lord. I pray that we will be totally focused on the Lord Jesus, our eyes fixed on Him. Let Your love, Father, shower over us. We are a hungry people, Lord, and we want to sit at the table with You. We love You and praise You for inviting us to Your table of mercy and grace. In Jesus' name, amen.

Chapter 3

WORLDVIEW SHAKEDOWN

by Greg Boyd

IN THE LATE 1980s AND early 90's I had a few experiences that rocked my world. For the first time in my life, I encountered real, overt cases of demonization. The first time was in the late 80's and then four times in the span of three weeks in 1991. Probably they are minor to what some people have encountered, but by my standards, they were freakoutishville. They blew my brain away; and what it did for me was make the reality of the demonic something that was tangible. Up to that point I was a Bible-believing Christian, and I believed in the reality of evil, the reality of demonic forces, and principalities and powers. But it's one thing to believe theoretically in something and it's something quite different to actually live as though it was true. So I had this theoretical belief, but it didn't impact the way I lived very much.

These experiences jarred my view of the world to the point I needed to try to figure things out. I needed to find a way of making sense out of them. I started going to conferences and reading books and all sorts of other things to try to really make sense of these experiences. Research opened me up to other sorts of experiences around the world, and it really put the problem of evil at the forefront of my mind. The problem of evil had always been there to some degree but now it became intense.

How can the world be such a nightmare if it's created and sustained by God? How is evil—and not just a little bit of evil, but demonic evil—possible when we have a world that was created and is sustained by an all-good and all-powerful God? So I went back to Scripture and looked at the acts of Jesus and theology in a different way—with a warfare worldview, as if biblical events were caught in the crossfire of a cosmic war.

Some people have an idea that theology is sort of an academic exercise in futility and to a certain degree, maybe even to a large degree, I have to agree with that assessment. Having read a good deal of theology in my life, I would conservatively estimate that three quarters of it is rather pointless, if not meaningless. Having said that though, I believe that our ideas, especially theological ideas, have import in our lives. They impact how we look at things, how we respond to things.

You have a theology whether you know it or not. The question is, did you choose that theology or did it choose you? Most people just sort of inherit a theology from the songs they hear or from a sermon they heard or something or other, and some of that can be really good; but some of it maybe is not good and it affects the way you view God and the way you respond to suffering and evil. Theology affects everything.

We are all wired differently. Some people are much more motive-driven. Others are more cerebral-driven, but all of us need to have some degree of congruency in the narrative that we live in and that's what theology is all about.

For me, it's more of a compulsive thing. The mood that I'm in at any given moment has more to do with how ideas are lining up within my head than anything to do in the external world. It took my wife about ten years to understand that I can be grouchy and it has nothing to do with her or our circumstances; rather, it's because something isn't lining up in my head. On the other hand, things can be going absolutely miserable, but I'm very happy because all of a sudden the coin in my mind fell into the slot. That can be a curse, but it can also be a gift in that I enjoy taking theological concepts and wrestling with them and asking the question, how can this be?

What makes this such an important issue is this: if we're not aware that there is a war going on, a cosmic battle that we are caught up in, then what can happen, and tends to happen, and more often than not has happened throughout church history, is that God gets blamed for a whole lot of the stuff that the devil does, or that principalities and powers do, or that evil people do, or for things that just happen.

If we don't have an understanding of the conflict that we are involved in, then we tend to think that God is just up there pulling all the strings and since the world, it turns out, is not all that nice of a place, it's easy to infer that God is not all that nice. It's easy to feel a moral obligation not to believe in God. In fact, I would say that most of the atheists I've met in my life reject a god that, if that was the only option on the table, I would also reject.

It's really not a question of believing in God or not. The question is, what god do you believe in? If people really have an accurate understanding of who God is, if their picture of God is based on Jesus Christ dying on the cross for the very people who crucified Him, praying with His last breath for the Father to forgive them—if that is our picture of God, then even if a person rejects believing in God, they ought to feel bad about it. It ought to be like, *Gosh, I wish that was true but it's not.* As it is, most people who reject a belief in God have a perverted picture of God that is monstrous. That picture of God is an inference based on the belief that since God is all-powerful and all-good and created this world, therefore He's responsible for everything that happens, even the kidnapping of little children and earthquakes that bury thousands of people alive and so on and so on. That god can't be all good if he did exist and so many people decide it's easier to not believe than to believe.

Let's talk about the *blueprint worldview* and the *warfare worldview*. I contrast these two, and I'm painting with very broad strokes. These can be infinitely nuanced if you're in a roomful of PhD's; but for our purposes, it is sufficient to paint with broad strokes.

Blueprint Worldview

By the blueprint worldview, I refer to the idea that everything follows a divine blueprint. There's a blueprint in Heaven and everything that takes place in time, everything that unfolds in history, is the working out of that blueprint. Everything was pre-settled ahead of time. And so in the blueprint worldview, everything happens for a specific, divine reason. God has a reason behind everything that happens.

I noticed one day a poster about a young girl who was kidnapped and murdered, and there was a reward for information leading to who did it. I think she was about 12 years old, a beautiful young lady. In the blueprint worldview, God has a reason for what happened. And since God is all good, the reason must be good, right? So if somehow it's good that a girl got kidnapped and killed, then it would be bad if she didn't get kidnapped and killed or at least less good, and you would have to say that about every particular evil in all of history.

The blueprint worldview considers every child who gasped for air as they were being incinerated in Hitler's gas chambers as dying a good death. And somehow the kidnapping, mutilation, and raping of little children contributes to the goodness of the universe and glorifies God. Ultimately, everything happens for a specific, divine reason, and whether people believe or not, everything follows the divine blueprint. So even those who ultimately reject God and go to hell, well that's all for a good, divine reason and God is glorified by their eternal torture.

Now you can begin to understand why some people think, *You know what, I can't believe in that kind of god.* The blueprint worldview holds that everything happens for a specific, divine reason.

Warfare Worldview

What I call the warfare worldview holds that the ultimate reason for evil lies in wills other than God's will. In the warfare worldview, the belief is that God created the cosmos but populated the universe with free agents, angelic and human, and maybe other sorts as well, for all we know. And because there is free will, these agents can align their wills with God or not. In the warfare worldview—at least the Christianized version of the warfare worldview—all evil, which by definition I'll later argue, is what is contrary to God's will. All evil originates in wills other than God's; angelic, human, and otherwise. Ultimately, all that is wrong with this universe is a result of those wills choosing contrary to God's will.

The Christian West tends toward the blueprint worldview. It permeates everything, even in the secular realm today. Almost everyone says, "Oh, nothing happens by accident. There's a reason for everything. God's timing is always right on time." If that is true, every child who was gassed or raped was right on time, right? God specifically chose that little girl to be tortured in that particular way. Do you really want to go there? But this sort of quasi-fatalism permeates many societies.

The warfare worldview has actually been the more common worldview throughout history. It is a piece of common knowledge that this world is all messed up. Different cultures have different stories about how it got messed up, but they have a common understanding that something is wrong and it has to do with forces in the spiritual realm. They all have an idea of good and bad angels and a large part of primordial religion is trying to figure out how to get the good spirits on your side and how to ward off the bad spirits and so on and so on, but we in the West tend to have this blueprint worldview that everything has a divine purpose.

In the warfare worldview—this is an important distinction—it's not that God causes all that comes to pass for a divine purpose. This is the view I'm defending. *It's not that God causes everything to come to pass for a divine purpose, but God brings divine purpose to everything that comes to pass.*

Some people are really committed to a blueprint worldview, and they accuse me of advocating a world that's out of control, chaotic, where things happen for no good reason, and God can't be assured a victory—and that's all nonsense. If you hold, as I do, that God is infinitely intelligent, then there's nothing that happens that catches God off guard. In fact, God has a plan for everything that happens, and God has a way, according to Romans 8:28. It is a plan to say, "OK, given that happened, even if it's against His will—and a whole lot that happens in this world is—I believe, He still has been preparing a plan for it for all eternity."

It's like a chess game. If you are playing against God in chess, you're going to lose because whatever move you make, He's been looking at that very move from the beginning of the game as though you had to make it. You could have made any other move and the same thing would be true. So there will be checkmate. Whatever move you make plays into His ultimate victory, and so as things unfold in this world, He's got a plan in place. He brings a purpose to everything: to bring good out of evil—but He doesn't cause the evil. If He was the cause of the evil and He's all good, well then it wouldn't really be evil—and therein lies the problem of the blueprint worldview.

Blueprint Worldview Challenges

The blueprint worldview renders moral responsibility unintelligible, I would argue. I don't usually quote *The New York Times* when talking theology, but recently there was an incredible article about some neurological studies regarding free will. What the studies revealed is that when people believed in fatalism, believed they really didn't have a choice, they tended to behave less ethically than when they believed they had a free choice— and that stands to reason. When people believe in fatalism, they tend not to hold themselves or other people responsible for what they do. Why? Because they believe that they could not do otherwise. A person who could not do otherwise is a person who can't be held responsible for what they do.

For example, if somebody is being tried for robbing a bank, and it turns out that somebody planted a microchip in their brain and was controlling every neuron in their brain from a distance and made them rob the bank, you would certainly blame the person who implanted the microchip and controlled the person rather than the person who was controlled.

So also, if God is in any sense the One who decrees that all evil comes to pass the way it comes to pass, how are people responsible for what comes to pass? How is it that I'm responsible for any evil that I do if God is the One who ordained me to do it, and I could not do otherwise?

And so what you have in the entire Church's traditions are concepts like, God ordains whatever comes to pass including all evil, in such a way that He is all holy for ordaining the evil, while the people who carry out what God ordained them to do are responsible for the evil they brought about. I've always wondered, *What does that mean?* I cannot find any analogy for someone being exhaustively determined to do something in such a way that they are responsible for what they did and whoever or whatever determined them to do it is not responsible. In any court of law that I can think of, the person would not be responsible if they were controlled or determined by someone outside of them. So it renders moral responsibility unintelligible.

For that reason, it tarnishes God's character. If God is in any sense behind all the evil in the world, it can't help but tarnish His character. Really, why do you even need satan if God is already doing all the evil? Satan just sort of becomes a puppet on God's hand, and there's no way to make coherent the idea that satan is doing all the evil stuff.

And finally, the blueprint worldview creates the theology of resignation rather than revolt. This is the practical fallout. When you believe that everything is just sort of happening—going according to plan even though the plan maybe stinks—you develop a *que sera sera* (what will be will be) attitude.

Warfare Worldview Realities

Our war is unlike any kind of ordinary human war. It's not against flesh and blood (see Eph. 6:12). If your opponent has flesh and blood, it's not your enemy. Our battle is against the principalities and powers, and the way that we do war is not by hatred, violence, or anything of the sort. The opposite is true; the way we do war is by loving everyone, blessing, praying for, and doing good toward those who persecute us. That is, in fact, our warfare. The way we fight principalities and powers is by loving those who are unlovable, those who are against us, and putting on display the character of our God and His Kingdom because His character is revealed on Calvary. He died for His enemies. He could have called legions of angels, could have called them in a second.

We do warfare by relinquishing power we could have used against our enemies and instead we use the power of God for them. We come under them. We die for them. We believe for them. In doing that, we're resisting the principalities and powers. The way we do warfare against the principalities and powers is by refusing to make humans our enemies. I'm convinced that the main reason we make humans our enemies is because we're acquiescing to the principalities and powers who specialize in playing us against one another, especially in the Church where there are so many fights. We're not spending enough time fighting off the real enemy, so we shoot at each other. For more thoughts about this subject, please read my book *God at War.*

Those of us in Western culture are conditioned to read the Bible in a certain way and it tends to be a blueprint way. In fact, many of the translations of the Bible tend toward a blueprint worldview versus other ways because this view conditions us. This is part of our inheritance, so we miss a lot of the insightful stuff the Bible has to say about God's conflict with evil.

It's almost as if there is a force of evil that's almost like gravity, and God is the One who holds things together by the power of His Word (see Heb. 1:3). He's the force of good against the perpetual force of evil. If God withdraws His hand even for a second, things fall into decay, into nothingness. I think this is what happened with the Flood. I think, in fact, most of the judgments in the Bible are about God withdrawing His hand. He doesn't have to do anything destructive. He just says OK, destruction is going to take place, and boom, there it is. It's part of the warfare motif.

The ultimate canvas against which the narrative of Scripture is painted, I submit, is a warfare narrative. It's not just a story about what God does, what God decrees. It's about how God brings about His will on earth as it is in Heaven despite the fact that there's opposition to His will in the heavenlies and on earth. It's a warfare narrative and mindset.

When you live as though everything is happening according to plan, you tend to live in what I call a vacation mindset as opposed to a warfare mindset. When you're on vacation it's appropriate to avoid as much conflict as possible, seek as much pleasure as possible, to enjoy yourself as much as possible, and to keep problems at bay as much as possible. That's what you do on vacation, and the Lord knows we all need vacations. But if you're in battle—if you're over in the Middle East or some other war zone—and you're in the midst of bullets flying and bombs exploding, that's not the time you want to be as comfortable as possible, enjoying pleasure as much possible, and running from conflict. No! You're in a war.

What's appropriate when you're on vacation is totally inappropriate when you're in a state of war. Now ask the question, which mindset do we Americans most tend toward? We live as though it is always appropriate to look out for number one. I want my best life now. I want as nice a house as possible, as much comfort as possible, as many conveniences as possible, as little warfare as possible. I want my loved ones and I to have nice things, and we run from conflict. I like when Jesus tells us to set up our tents at the gates of hell, to storm the gates of hell. Rather, we like to storm into our gated communities and stay in them—live in our nice little American mirages.

This is why ideas are important. What mindset do you live in? Do you live in vacation mode, looking out for number one. Or do you live in a warfare narrative where right now there are bombs and bullets going off all over the place and you realize that you have a job to do. Choosing the mindset you live in determines your effectiveness for the Kingdom of God.

Hang On to Jesus

In a world that is caught in a war zone, the only way we can even know what is coming from the enemy and what's coming from God is by knowing the character of God, and for that we have to hang tightly onto the person of Jesus Christ. All other things being equal, if Jesus didn't do it, we shouldn't suppose God has done it, because Jesus is our key, our clue to what God is like.

So now I'm going to layout a theodicy—an explanation for the problem of evil. This is my telling of a story that is deeply rooted in Scripture. I believe that there are five ideas, or theses, that account for how an all-powerful, all-good God could create a world that is now caught in cosmic war, a world that is a nightmarish place much of the time.

THESIS 1. LOVE REQUIRES FREEDOM.

Love for created beings requires freedom. God's goal in creating the world—this is the assumption I'm working on; I think it's a good one based on Scripture—was to manifest His love and invite other created beings, angels and humans, into His love; but if there is going to be love, there has to be choice. There has to be free will. You can use coercive force, what I call Neanderthal power, to accomplish a lot of things, but you can't use it to get someone to love you. I don't care how strong you are, how forceful you are, how controlling you are, and Lord knows a lot of men try, but you cannot Neanderthal your way into a love relationship. It either comes freely or it doesn't come at all, no matter how sophisticated the controlling power might be.

Suppose, for example, I were a mad scientist and I was able to invent a computer chip that once placed in the brain would control every neuron in a person's brain. I could program it so that everything that happened in the brain would be my doing and it was so sophisticated I could slip it into someone's ear. Note: this is material also found in my books *Is God to Blame?* and even more deeply in *Satan and the Problem of Evil*.

Now imagine I put the chip into my wife's ear while she was sleeping and it's programmed to produce the perfect wife. Because it controls every neuron in her brain, and since every thought we think is simply neurons firing in our brain, she wouldn't even know it. Every thought she would think would be the thoughts that I wanted her to think via the computer chip. So as she wakes up in the morning, she is the perfect wife—which I would hardly be able to tell the difference from anyway [wink].

Her first thought upon waking would be, *Whoa, what a blessed woman I am. I'm married to such a hunk of a spiritual man.* Then she would look at me with ravished, hungry eyes like she always does in the morning. I would have to rip myself away from her to go to work. When I come home that evening, she would have a delicious dinner made for me and be dressed in my favorite outfit. She would love on me, saying all the right things, thinking all the right thoughts, having all the right loving words and actions—she would be the perfect wife.

Now here's the thing. Would I be satisfied with that? Heck yes! No, no matter how base I am, and I can be very base, after a day...a week...a year tops...a decade for sure, I would know that her behavior isn't real love. Everything my wife is feeling, thinking, doing, and saying is really me doing it to myself via the computer chip. This isn't real love. It would not be satisfying. Shelly wouldn't be giving me anything I didn't already have. It's a sick version of an egotistical me, me loving myself through her. I would be using her.

If I want real love from my wife or from anybody, they have to have the ability to say no to it. It's an intuitive truth. And better to have imperfect real love that is chosen than a coerced love. Coerced love is simply puppetville or the Stepford Wives. God could have created a Stepford Wife world. He could have had a bride who was perfect. The Stepford Bride of Christ. We would have been so perfect, we would have never sinned, and we would have faithfully worshiped Almighty God. But that is a mannequin world. It isn't real. It isn't personal interaction.

For personal love, there has to be choice.

For example, God says in Deuteronomy 30, "I've set before you life and death, blessings and curses, now choose life so that you and your children may live." Choose life. God wants us to choose life, but as the Israelites proved oh so well, you can choose death; and when you choose death, that's what comes to you.

It says in Luke 7, by refusing to be baptized by John the Baptist, the Pharisees and the lawyers rejected God's purpose for them. That shows us that God has a purpose for your life and you can accept it or you can reject it, and if you reject it, that's not God's purpose for your life. No, His purpose for your life was to accept it. This idea that everything goes according to God's will simply can't account for the fact that people reject God's will and the angels reject God's will. That's the very definition of sin and this motif runs throughout the Bible.

THESIS 2. FREEDOM REQUIRES RISK.

If I am going to take the microchip out of my wife's brain in order for her to love, that means that there is a risk she might choose not to love or at least not love me perfectly. There is possibly going to be some pain involved in this move, but I would rather have imperfect and perhaps painful real love than imperfect but controlled perfect love, because that is no love at all.

So freedom requires risk. If God creates a universe populated with free agents, angelic and human, there's a risk that things might not go according to His perfect plan, which as we now know is in fact what happened; and we find this throughout the Bible. At various times, the Lord regrets things. He made decisions but, because of human decisions, things don't turn out the way He had hoped.

He made Saul king of Israel; Saul turned out to be a terrible king. In First Samuel 15, God said He regretted having made Saul king of Israel. Things didn't work out, there's a risk involved, and sometimes the negative side of risk prevails. The

Bible reveals that God gets frustrated and grieved. For example, in Isaiah 5, He is disappointed. This is an incredible passage where the Lord says, "I made you into a garden"—He's talking about Israel—"and I took care of you. I did everything I could possibly do to take care of you and yet instead of producing good fruit like I thought you would, you produced this wild fruit. What more could I do for you?" he asks, "than what I've already done." There was a risk, because Israel was populated with free agents. God can do everything God can do and yet we still have the ability to say no to Him. The Lord regrets the way things turn out; and *if we understand that freedom involves risk, we can begin to understand how God is not culpable for the evil in His creation.*

Some people will say things like, "Well, God is still responsible for all the evil in the world because even if He made us free, He's still the One who did it." But if there's a real risk involved, then you can understand how God is no more responsible for the evil that we produce than a parent is responsible for the evil their children produce, assuming that they were as good as parents as possible. There are parents who abuse their kids and that partly explains why the kids turn out a certain way; but other times, kids can be raised ideally and perfectly and they turn out to be absolutely murderous. No one can say it's the parents' fault because they brought the kid into the world.

No, when you enter love, there's a risk. When you bring a child into the world, there's a risk. When you get married, there's a risk. Anytime we love, there's a risk. It might backfire because there are free agents involved, but I'm sure you agree that it's worth it, because we keep playing the game. It is worth it not to isolate yourself and go into a subhuman, very lonely and miserable existence.

So God sets up a world where we can be disappointed if we choose our way instead of His way. Allow me to paraphrase what He says in Jeremiah: *I thought that after I poured love and kindness in you in the desert and the wilderness you would turn to Me. I thought that after I showered you with grace you would turn to Me, but you didn't.* So here's a God, the omnipotent, all-powerful God who creates a world in which He can be disappointed, in which He regrets. He creates a world in which He can get frustrated and grieve.

In Ezekiel 22, He is very frustrated. He says to Ezekiel, "You know your judges were judging unjustly and you don't care for the poor, you don't care for the needy"—which is always the main reason why God judges nations in the Bible—and He says, "This judgment was coming on you and I tried to find someone to stand in the gap to repair the wall to prevent this from happening, but I could find no one." God didn't want to bring judgment even though they deserved it; He looked but couldn't find anybody. This is a God who was grieving; He was frustrated. An omnipotent God tries to do something that ends up not being done. How is that possible? Well, if we have free will, and free will involves a risk, you can begin to understand how that is possible.

In Romans 10:21, the Lord says, *"All day long I have held out My hands to a disobedient and obstinate people."* All day long God is saying come to Me, turn to Me, choose life—but we don't, and that's the risk He took when He created agents who are free. God, throughout the Bible, tested people to see whether they were going to be faithful or not. There's a risk involved in this and sometimes they don't pass His test—sometimes we don't pass His tests.

God creates us free because freedom is the prerequisite to love—and freedom always involves an element of risk.

THESIS 3. RISK REQUIRES MORAL RESPONSIBILITY.

It's like this. Love is the ability to bless another, to ascribe worth to another, which I think is probably the most basic definition you could give to describe agape love. Jesus gave His life for us, sacrificed for us, ascribed worth to us. First John 3:16 says that's what love is.

So if love is the ability to ascribe worth to another, and love involves freedom to do the opposite of love, that means I have to have the power to detract worth from you. If I have the power to love you and ascribe worth to you, and I have to be free and freedom involves risk, that means there is always a risk that I could detract worth from you as well. I could harm you. If I have the power to bless you, then I have the power to harm you—that is built into the very nature of love. If God is going to create a world where love is possible, that means He's going to create a world where we are to some degree morally responsible for one another. We have the ability to love one another and we have to have the ability to harm one another.

For example, consider the atrocious things that happen such as the mother who drowned her five children in the bathtub. Everyone wondered how that was possible. *God, why didn't You stop her? Why would God allow a mother to do this?* And I submit to you that it's not because the world is a better place with these five children gone. We live in a world where a mother can give life and love her five children, but she is just as capable of killing her five children as she is capable of loving her five children.

Does it ever freak you out when you are driving down the road and all of a sudden you realize that if the driver coming toward you on the other side of the road turned the wheel an inch in your direction you could have a head-on crash and be killed? It's weird how iffy life is. One inch, just like that. It's crazy. Or if you fell asleep for just a second. Or if another driver drank alcohol before getting into the car that's heading your way. Our lives hang in the balance of one another, and it has to be that way. If we're going to be people who are capable of loving one another, blessing one another, choosing the good, we must realize that each of us can also choose the evil.

So love requires moral responsibility; but notice that when *I use my free will for evil*, that's about me, not about God. This is so important. For instance, I can decide to pick up a rock and pound my neighbor in the head several times causing irreversible brain damage; I have that power. I have the power to do that because I also have the power to bless my neighbor as well. I have the power to love; I have the power to destroy.

You don't have to ask God, *why did I do that?* or even, *God, why did You allow that,* as though God wanted that to happen. It makes more sense to ask, *God, why did You create a world where agents have free will so they can do that kind of thing?* That makes sense and that's what we're addressing right now, but once you grant that God has a reason for giving us free will, you don't have to then go further and ask God for the specific reasons why we use our free will the way we do. If I bash my neighbor in the head, that's about me, not God. God's given me the power to do that because otherwise I couldn't love my neighbor—and that's about God.

That's what it means to have moral responsibility. We go down the wrong track when we start blaming God for things that free agents do, human and angelic. You might as well blame the parents or grandparents for everything that a child does, but because we have free will, then to some degree the buck stops with us.

Thesis 4. Moral responsibility is proportionally balanced.

If you accept that moral responsibility is proportionally balanced, it explains why some have power to harm so many. For example, a person could ask the question, "Why is it that we have the ability to harm one another?" This person could accept the answer that it has to do with free will, but what do you do in cases where Hitler had the ability to kill 6 million people and Stalin was responsible for 30 million deaths?

Or think about satan, the high-ranking, maybe the highest-ranking, archangel who turned against God, and has, in some ways, been responsible for all the evil that has transpired throughout history. Why does he have so much authority? It seems like bad management, doesn't it? I submit that the extent to which we have the power to harm another is balanced by the extent to which we have an ability to bless another. Think of descending proportionalities, the higher I can soar, the lower I can fall. The bigger they are, the harder they fall, or like Milton said about satan in *Paradise Lost*, as high as he could have soared, so low he fell.

There is a principle of proportionality. Every gift you have can be used for good or it can be used for evil, and the stronger the gift is, the more the potential for evil. That's why I think there's more of a bounty on your head. We say that all people are created equal, and that's all true in terms of how much God loves us, but in every other respect it's not. We are all very, very different. None of us are equal in the same way. We all have various gifts and we can use those gifts for good or we can use those gifts for evil. It takes a genius to be really, really evil. If you study Nazi Germany, you will see what happens when genius turns evil. It's just incredible. And what we see in Adolf Hitler is simply the reverse of Mother Teresa. How one human being can be used to make such a difference to millions and millions of people is the principle of proportionality.

It's important to remember that never is responsibility isolated to one individual. It may look like this, but there are always other things that come into play. For example, Hitler was, we'll assume, the main human responsible for the Holocaust, but he couldn't have done what he did unless there were hundreds of people, brilliant people, willing to work with him. The responsibility was shared, and they couldn't have done what they did unless there were millions of people willing to at least look the other way, if not cooperate with them to some degree, for their own benefit. And they couldn't have done what they did unless there was a long history, four centuries, of anti-Semitism being preached in Prussia in Jesus' name. Martin Luther bears a lot of responsibility for that long history of anti-Semitism, but even that wouldn't have been as bad as it was if it wasn't for principalities and powers that were fueling this kind of hatred in the spiritual realm.

So, in my opinion, when you are looking at who is responsible for the holocaust, one can say that yes, Hitler was responsible, but not Hitler alone. The whole inner circle of the Nazi party was responsible, and then the larger circle of the Nazi party, and then all of Germany, and then the whole Western world, who to some degree let it happen. And the Church to some degree is responsible, as well as those who kept anti-Semitism alive for four centuries, and then the principalities and powers also had a hand in the deaths of millions. Still, it has to be proportionality balanced.

THESIS 5. MORALLY RESPONSIBLE FREEDOM IS IRREVOCABLE.

If you're trying to make sense out of evil in the world, I think this is absolutely essential to understand: morally responsible freedom is irrevocable, and I'm saying this in principle. There are all sorts of qualifications that we don't need to get into, but moral responsibility has got to be irrevocable by definition.

Let's go back to my wife. Suppose I put a chip in her brain to control all the neurons. For two months she's the Stepford Wife. I get tired of that. I want her to choose to love me so I don't want to control her mind anymore. On the other hand, I really like her being a Stepford Wife, so instead of controlling everything she does, I simply create a program that will revoke her free will whenever it's going to do anything other than what I want her to do. Have I changed anything by doing that? No.

If you give people free will to go this way or that way, the choice is theirs. God can't revoke their ability to go that way simply because He doesn't like it. Why? Because He gave them free will and free will is the ability to go this way or that way. It's no different than saying, if God is going to create a bachelor, he can't be married. If God is going to create two adjacent mountains, they have to have a valley in between. If God is going to create a circle, it can't have three straight sides. You get the point.

To make creatures free means they have the power to go this way or that way, which means God has to put up with it to some degree, put up with it and work around it; God has to use wisdom, not just power. It's not a question of how much power God has. God has the power to revoke free will, but if he revoked it, He clearly wouldn't have created the kind of world that He did create, which is a world of free agents who have the power to choose His way or their way.

• • •

Father, please clarify our understanding of You. Give us a picture of You, a mental picture of You that is accurate or at least pointing in the right direction, that to some degree captures the infinite beauty of Your character. And free us, Lord God; power us into people who understand the world is at war and that we have an important role to play. Father, I thank You for trusting us to be led by the power of Your Spirit, a bride who reigns with You. I pray, Lord God, that we would just not be deluded and deceived by the American dream or any other version of the vacation mindset that causes us to live as though this life were the primary thing, let alone the only thing. Lord, help us to be a people whose eyes are set on eternity while dedicated to loving those around us. In Jesus' name we pray, amen.

Chapter 4

RAISING THE DEAD

by Rolland Baker

HEIDI, MY WIFE, AND I have a ministry in Mozambique, and the poor pastors there come to our Bible school and don't know a thing. They don't know the difference between the Old and New Testament, law and grace, where Israel is located, or what the Jordan is. They have no idea. They're uneducated. All they know how to do is *raise the dead*! But we put them through discipleship, get them to read books, hear lectures, and see enough DVDs that they can start doubting God—like many do in the West. That is not actually what we do, but I tell that story as a prelude of what I have to share with you about furious love, about how people are desperate for a crazy, wild, and furious God encounter.

A medical team from Harvard University came to our ministry in Cabo Delgado, Mozambique, after learning that deaf people were being healed. Every deaf person who came to our bush conferences would be healed. And it doesn't matter who prays—little kids, our students, pastors, Heidi, me, it doesn't matter. There's an open heaven over Cabo Delgado for deaf people. The skeptical medical team came to Pemba, Mozambique with a load of instruments to check ears and eyesight, and they went with Heidi way out in the bush to a typical bush conference.

They got all their instruments out, and Heidi called for the deaf to come forward. They didn't come right away because they couldn't hear, but then their friends and family pushed them out. They stood in the dirt, waiting, looking numb. The team got out their instruments and performed pre-tests. They had all the graphs and the needle was going up and down; everything was recorded and digitized. Heidi started praying for the first one—pop, she could hear. Second one—pop, he could hear. Third one, fourth one, fifth one, sixth one, and the seventh one—they all dropped on their knees and wept. The team published their findings in a major American medical journal. I took that report—which I have on the Internet with all the pages, the graphs, the details, and all the footnotes—and I handed it to people, to friends, and to doubters; but human nature is just incredibly hard to penetrate.

You can hand proof to somebody and they may say, "Well, I don't know, sounds pretty biased to me. I'll bet you if you took a team out there from some other viewpoint, and they brought their instruments, their results would show whatever they wanted to show." Jesus said some could watch the dead rise and still not believe. And there are some who can even be resurrected themselves and not appreciate it.

Some of our new pastors, usually two or three in every class, have already raised the dead. We have seen people raised from the dead, and it excites the whole village and fires up everybody. They charge out into the bush, pastors headed in all directions for 100 miles, barefoot and without food, just so on fire for God

Raising the Dead

that they start churches in every village that doesn't have one. But the person who was raised from the dead may not be all that excited. It's curious, the reactions.

Fire, fervor, temperature, emotion, pleasure, joy, rejoicing, abundant life, initiative, and energy are all gifts from God. Just because we know our doctrines and sing the songs and hear the stories and say we believe and go to church does not mean we are full of life. People think it's irreverent for us to get all excited and fall over and laugh like silly people in church. I'll tell you what's irreverent—to just sit there!

Unfortunately, humans have an ability, a supernatural ability, to be bored by God. They have an ability to sit in church and be unmoved. They have an ability to wake up in the morning and think, *OK, just another day.* Many people don't understand the value in sitting and laughing and enjoying God. They don't get excited. And then I have had other people come up and say, "I haven't laughed in years; fork it over!"

Jesus said unless you become like a little child you don't get into the Kingdom (see Matt. 18:3). It took me about ten years of systematic theological study to get this childlike. It takes that long of a study to figure out where it isn't.

Mysteries

After a meeting at Cambridge University, two PhDs came running up to me. One was a student of Stephen Hawking, considered the world's foremost theoretical physicist and familiar with the mysteries of the universe. The first one said, "Rolland, as educated as you are, how is it possible that you can just relax and be at peace and content with God with so many unanswered questions...with so many unresolved issues. There are so many tensions in the Scripture. How can you just sit and enjoy the

• 77 •

presence of God?" The other guy ran up and threw himself at my feet and said, "I gotta have what you have!" They both had PhDs, they both were educated, and both had a totally different response to what I shared with them that day.

Now the fact is, there are huge mysteries concerning God and the spiritual realm. The ultimate mysteries I ponder include, *Where did God come from? Why is there a God? How could He have always existed? Why is that? In fact, why is there anything? Why is anything the way it is? How did anything get to be anything?*

There are unbelievable, huge mysteries; the nature of time, the nature of eternity, every last issue in the Bible, every last biblical, spiritual principle has various facets and dimensions. They need multiple models for us to understand. God's perfection requires a spectrum of models, and understandings, and balances, and sides of the coin; theology can get intensely intellectual and as deep as you want to get and it's all true. That's the fantastic thing about it; the pursuit of truth never ends.

For people who like to think it's exhilarating because there is always more to think about and more to pursue, we can also relate to Psalm 131. O God, I don't think about great, and marvelous, and difficult, and ponderous things that I don't understand. I just quiet myself like a little baby against its mother, and I just relax and I just trust like a little baby.

Isn't that fantastic? We have the choice. Any time we want, we can pursue truth and we can ask and discuss things with God all day long. One of my favorite things to do is walk for hours on the beach in Africa and discuss things with God, anything and everything that's deep and heavy on my heart, to the limit of my appetite and ability. It is so exhilarating; but when I'm done, I'm done. And even though we have tens of thousands of children and pastors and churches and problems and crises to deal with all the time, anytime I want I can say, "Jesus, it's all Yours. I give my cares to You." I don't understand much of anything, but to have a God-given gift of trust without understanding, without knowing what you're doing, when you're not in control, when you don't feel like you amount to anything, when you don't feel like you can get anywhere, and you have zero confidence in yourself, you realize we have a perfect Savior. The most blessed people in the world are those who have been given faith in the one and only perfect Savior.

And God just loves to give this kind of faith as a free gift to the least of these, to the most unlikely on the planet, to the least educated, to the most un-influential, to people at the bottom of the mountain. He loves to show Himself, reveal Himself to the humble. God gives grace to the humble and is opposed to the proud. What a relief.

The Richest People

Do you know who are the richest people in the world? It's not the people who have the most; it's *the people who need the least to be happy, content, and godly.* That's great gain, the New Testament says. To have nothing like Sadhu Sundar Singh, the early apostles, or many of our pastors in Africa, to have nothing but the clothes on your back, a walking stick, and a Bible—to set out without food, without money, and be happy and full of God. These pastors are raising the dead and healing the sick; they go into villages that have never heard the Gospel, encounter demon-possessed cannibals, and kick out all the demons— and people hear about it. These people will then walk all day long with a sick friend on their back, barefoot, and waist-deep in mud without food because they heard Jesus was in such and such a village.

You can build a big, beautiful building and dress like a man of God with your heavy robes and gold crosses and all of that, and very few people will come to hear you. You have your ceremonies, choirs, and music, but very few people will come. But if they hear God is in town, all they need to know is that Jesus is real, loves them, can help them with supernatural power, and that they can trust Him, then they flock around you. They will stream in from all over. That's what they need to know, a real, actually alive God.

The best thing about God is that He is God. He's not some theoretical construct, some belief system, some tradition that God handed down, or something that a pastor is trying to push down our throats. God is not some Western civilization product; He's not an Eastern tradition. He is God. There is only one of Him.

I'm thinking of some desperate guy who stood up in a Hindu temple in India and saw 10,000 gods carved into stones all around. His wife was sick and dying and he wanted to know, "OK, come on you guys. If any one of you is alive, would the real one please stand up? Any of you? Anyone?" Jesus is the only One who ever shows up. The wife is healed, the husband becomes an evangelist, and that's that. It's really that simple.

Why?

So, why are you here? Why did God make you? Sometimes we think God exists for us. Actually, we exist for Him. He made us for His own pleasure. He absolutely did not want to be stuck in Heaven forever with nothing but angels around, walking along empty gold streets, and gazing at a whole bunch of mansions.

Heidi and I have been on our deathbeds many times. It gets boring. We have been sick with everything from myalgic encephalitis (chronic fatigue), multiple sclerosis, blood poisoning, pneumonia, incurable staff infections, and on and on. I had an incurable blood disease when I came out of Indonesia. We were penniless and in the cheapest ward of the Queen Elizabeth Hospital in Hong Kong; people were dying in the beds next to me. They just left them there for hours because they didn't know whom to contact. And they didn't know what to do with me, so they put me under quarantine. I was tired of it and finally I said, "God, I want angels. I want angels all around my bed and I want out of here." I received a phone call that night from a friend in Hawaii who said, "Hey, I had a vision of angels around your bed all night." The next morning I was out of there.

But God wanted more than angels. Angels are fantastic, but there's something He wanted more. What does God do for His own self-satisfaction? In fact, what does God do in the morning? What is there to do if you are God? What does He do for His own pleasure? How does He satisfy His own heart? If you had all power, what would you do with it? You're sitting in the space of black nothingness around you, and you could make anything, create anything, do anything you wanted—what would you do with all your infinite creativity? What would you do?

Well, God spent millions of years thinking about it. What can I make? What can I look forward to? What can I create? What kind of situation can I come up with? What can I do with myself as God? How do I become happy? And He figured out… well, let's back up slightly. This gets into deep theology.

The Ultimate Creation—Relationship

What is God? I think fundamentally He's not just an impersonal object who is alone. God is love. He is relationship—Father and Son. That relationship is God. The more we study physical science and physics, the more we realize that's true in the physical world and quantum theory and so forth, everything is what it is only by virtue of its relationship with something else. There is no such thing as just you. The reality is your relationship with other people and that's what God is, He's relationship and that's what He wants. That's what He is.

So the most natural thing for Him to do is to create people, to create relationship; and after millions of years of thinking about it and summoning all of His creative powers, He comes up with the absolute best that He can possibly come up with—you.

We humans are the ultimate result of Almighty God's most infinite creativity, and He didn't just make us and say, "OK, now, let's just see how well you do and whether you love Me or not and if you were worth making." He actually created the relationship we have with Him—that's His ultimate creation.

God actually designs and creates our relationship with Him, and that is to the ultimate product of His creativity, which is designed to satisfy, first of all, Himself. Relationship. What a better creation that is than gold, money, objects, a Mercedes, prosperity, full bank accounts, positions, big church buildings, and favorite television shows, etc. Jesus asked, "Isn't life more than food and clothes and stuff?"

I want to add some balance to the whole renewal idea that 90 percent of sermons have to be about health and wealth. In Mozambique, we need health and wealth more than anyplace in the world. But you know what? You can't get health and wealth by trying to get health and wealth. In fact, you can't get anything from God unless it's God you want. You can talk about it. You can fleece the flock for your own gain, but you don't bring prosperity.

The ultimate product is relationship. We're not here to prove to the world we're the best. We're not here to take over. We're not here to dominate. We're not here to take the reins. We're not here to prove we're the top of the heap on everything. In fact, when you think about it, there's only room at the very top for One.

God loves to show His grace, His love, by reaching down to the most broken, the most unlikely, the people the world has no use for, and create out of them something for Himself and demonstrate His power, creativity, glory, and beauty, and by shear contrast shine the brightest in the darkest places. The richest people in Heaven are those who have shipped up the most treasure to Heaven instead of saving up treasure on earth. Some of the poorest in this world are going to be the greatest saints in Heaven with the most glory and the most reward. We need to turn everything upside down in the Church and be as unlike the world as absolutely possible.

So we need more than angels. God needs more than angels. He needs us. We are created because He Himself is thirsty for companionship, affection, honor, friendship, love, intimacy, somebody to talk to, somebody to enjoy life with, somebody to be free and happy with, and He's more childlike than we are. He jokes more than we do. He invented humor. It's not just a concession, you know, to poor humans who just can't handle life. It's not just a release for people who can't deal with reality. Joy is reality. Being happy and carefree like a child, enabled by God's grace and by the gift of the Holy Spirit to receive and to enjoy life, and to be full of His energy is reality. Joy is the energy of the Holy Spirit. I learned that from persecuted Christians in China.

We argue about whether or not there is going to be a tribulation. Are we going to have to suffer for three and one-half years or seven years or something like that? Well, the Christians I know in China went through 17 years of cultural revolution that exceeds anything I have read about in the Book of Revelation. It's a moot point. They have already tasted the worst the devil can do and they won. Wow, they won. That gives God glory.

For His Glory

What gives God glory? We can give God glory by succeeding, doing well, and prospering. We can use our gifts for Him. We can exercise goodness, righteousness, and our talents to express His beauty and that does give Him glory. But the question is, why are we here? Why are we left on earth? Why doesn't God just save us completely and take us to Heaven right now where things are easy? Why does it take so long for us to conquer the world and fix everything? I think He could fix the entire world overnight. I think He could feed every hungry person worldwide today. I think he could heal every AIDS victim in the entire world in one hour. He has that kind of power, but He doesn't do it.

For all the talk of miracles, the truth is that most people in most churches in most of the world don't see many; and even many who pray for miracles don't get them. How is that for an encouraging word? There's a reason for that. I have a theory that if God does something, He does it for a good reason; and if He doesn't do something, it's for a good reason. He is rational. I think He is perfectly rational, the most rational Person in the universe. He has reasons for what He does and doesn't do. I think relationship is His primary object, not just amazing people with magic tricks or providing whatever it is they want unless His priorities stand. He has priorities.

Is it always God's will to heal you? No. Why is that? There are good reasons. You might really need some adjustment somewhere in a way that's more important to God than your healing and more important for you, and more important for your future. He's a good God. He's a perfect God, and we are after the outcome of His dealings with us.

That's what Heidi and I have always prayed. She was one of the first people, maybe the only person, I've ever met who would pray, "God smash me, break me, discipline me, treat me like a real Dad until I am what You want. I don't care what it takes. I don't want any suffering that's not necessary. I don't want anything extra. I want it as easy as possible. I'm not into persecution for the fun of it. If there's any easier way....." It's like when Jesus prayed in Gethsemane, "God, if there's any other way, take this cup from me."

But God has a cup of both joy and suffering for us to drink and there's a reason for that. A lot of people at Church try to compartmentalize or divide the issue. There are people who preach revival and then there are people who preach that revival is not necessary—miracles and all of that are not so necessary. In fact, they say that they have never been that great, miracles have been exaggerated. The history of revival shows that they are not as wonderful as people think—there's a lot of corruption and mixture of spiritual issues. Even my own parents told me that. "Rolland, don't get so excited about the Indonesian revival, and go here and go there. They are rarely what you think they are, and they are usually a disappointment. Just get used to normal things. God uses normal people with normal talents, and that's what He does these days. Learn to accept that."

Then there's the other side that's talking about Heaven on earth, and we are on this side of the cross. Job didn't need to suffer if he had just known who he was and didn't trumpet his own righteousness. And Stephen didn't need to be stoned, and Paul didn't need to be shipwrecked and beaten within a stroke of death. And all 12 apostles didn't need to be martyred—we just know better now. We are here to take over and be masters of the planet. We are here to pray away every earthquake and every disease until this place is perfect like Heaven. That sounds good to me.

You know what? That's coming. It's coming. Paul said in Romans 8, if God did not spare His own Son but gave Him up for us, how will He not also along with Him give us all things? The time is coming when we will, in fact, rule, reign, be glorified, and possess all things; however, something else has to happen first. Now we get back to the idea of relationship. God wants relationship. He doesn't do miracles just to do miracles, just to prove to people what an amazing, powerful, and incredible God He is. He doesn't do it just to impress people. Neither would He do miracles if in any way they take away affection for Him; He's a jealous God.

Our Jealous God

He made you for Himself. He's not about to give you something that's going to take your affection away from Him in the slightest. Even the Old Testament says, God, don't give me so much that I forget you or so little that I'm bitter and steal. Give me the right amount that blesses me and keeps me close to you and in love with you.

He is after relationship, and He will do any miracle in the world toward that end, and He won't do anything if it's not toward that end. He is very selective about what He does and doesn't do. You can't make Him do things, and you shouldn't be interested in changing His will and making Him bend to what you think should be done. Jesus said His food was to do the will of His Father who sent Him. It was His thrill to do His Father's will. He never did anything unless it was the will of His Father. That sounds like a lot of control, but we totally underestimate the Holy Spirit. Where the Spirit of the Lord is—there is freedom. If God half controls you, you are half free. If He's not in control of you at all, you are a total slave of sin. If He's totally in control of you, you are completely free.

When you are so free that you cannot even believe you get to do what you were told to do, and your will and God's coincide perfectly, and you are just exalting because you just can't stand it you're so happy—that's when the Holy Spirit is 100 percent totally in control of you. That's how sovereignty works, and I like it.

Some people are outraged that we act so familiar with God, like He's a friend or something, like we actually know Him. They feel this way because they are distant from Him, scared, overwhelmed, they don't understand, can't feel His love, can't comprehend His grace—it can't be that easy, that simple, they reason. You Christians are just cheap; you're silly. I've got big problems, and you are acting childlike. I need a serious religion.

What helps you is to know God so well that you can be familiar with Him and be the kind of companion for Him that He's really hungering for, just like your own children. You want a relationship with your own children because you know how much you love them and it's your pleasure to do what they tell you—when you know it's in their best interest.

Revival

It's not my will to change God's will. That's not what I'm trying to do. But the other side of the coin, and there's always another side of the coin to make things perfect, is that God loves us to get so close and so familiar with Him that you can tell Him what to do. Jesus said, if My words abide in you, and you abide in Me, and you do what I tell you, you can ask anything in My name and I'll do it (see John 15:7). That's what I call revival, when God has His way. The Kingdom of God is wherever God has His way. What He wants is the same thing we want deep down—affection, companionship, romance, love, peace, joy in the Holy Spirit, without which no physical, outward miracle has any value whatsoever.

So in Mozambique we have learned not to chase miracles. We don't chase money, fundraising, influence, or prosperity. We don't chase anything but God. He is the full, entire, complete desire of our hearts. When we have Him, we have everything. We are totally rich. And we commit adultery the second our affections go somewhere else.

Do you realize you can commit adultery against God by loving your wife more than Him? Do you realize you can raise money for orphans and sell child sponsorships and have huge humanitarian aid projects and do incredible amounts of good and spend your wealth on medical research and AIDS and yet be committing adultery the whole time? Paul said in the Book of Romans, everything that does not proceed from faith is sin, and faith is total and complete trust in our God and perfect Savior so that He gets the credit for everything. Because we love Him, we want Him to get the credit.

How do you start a revival? About 15 years ago before we went to Mozambique, a pastor in San Francisco asked Heidi and me that question. Half joking, I said, "Oh, let's start by raising the dead." I had no idea at that time we would do exactly that. How do you start a revival in Mozambique? Well, first thing you need to do is have 500 years of slavery and colonialism just to make sure the people are humble. That's the first strategy. Then you need a long war against the colonists that kills half the men and plants three million land mines in your country. Then you need a civil war between the communists and the rebels that totally destroys the economy. Add to that some of the worst flooding in recorded history from three cyclones that brought rain for 40 days and 40 nights and washed out a third of the country so that almost half the kids couldn't find their parents. This happened in the year 2000 and made people so desperate for God that when we went into their refugee camps in the pouring rain and water the people were screaming to take the food, trucks, and aid. On top of that you need an AIDS epidemic, famines, and earthquakes. Now you have a country ready for revival.

But we don't need all that for revival. We only need a love for God. I know people who have endured persecution in China, like my father's vice principal in the first Bible school that he started after World War II. The communists came and took this man of God away, put him in prison, put his wife in another prison, and they didn't see each other for 22 years. I could go on and on about the many people who have suffered for Christ Jesus.

One time I was in a church in China. The pastor had come out of prison and had been tortured; the whole congregation was weeping. Why were they weeping? I thought they had such compassion for their pastor. They were so sorry for what happened to him. They were so sincere in their sorrow. But I found out later that they were weeping, sobbing their guts out, because they had not yet been considered worthy to suffer the same things.

There are people in this world who love God more than we can possibly imagine, and they have proven it; that is what God is after in this life. His primary purpose is not just to bless us and make everything easy. His primary purpose is to prove to the devil, the world, the angels, to Himself, and to everybody how much we love Him. The sufferings are not worthy to be compared to the glory that is to be revealed.

You are not subjected to anything you can't handle. He is going to prove that our faith is genuine and that our relationship with Him is real. It gives Him great glory on Judgment Day when God can say, "These are My people, and I will save them because they long for Me. They can't wait for Me to come, they love Me and have chosen Me in this life and chosen Heaven over their life on earth. They have given up everything on earth for Me, and if anyone loves the world or anything in it, the love of the Father is not in Him."

That's just to add some balance to the renewal. That's what He's after, to develop in us a relationship that has been proven to be real and satisfies Him and answers the accusations of the devil and the world and everybody around, and proves once and for all there's going to be such a display of the difference between good and evil. The quality of our relationship with God in this final struggle with the enemy will be enough proof to make clear, to establish beyond all doubt, the superiority of God's love and righteousness over evil.

That's what gives us the greatest possible resurrection. I don't know very many people anymore in the renewal whose hearts are up there where He is and their eyes and hearts are set on the things that are unseen, which are eternal and not the things that are seen, which are temporary. They want to lay up as much treasure in Heaven as possible, and they will suffer the loss of all things they consider rubbish in comparison to the value of knowing Christ Jesus as their Lord.

A Foretaste of Heaven

God blesses us along the way of life. He gives us down payments on Heaven. We love it when He gives us refreshments and blessings during our journey. There's a foretaste of Heaven, but if that is all it was, we wouldn't get a reward. Even sinners can enjoy and love people who love them and when they're prosperous and everything is fine. Even sinners can relax and be nice to people if people are nice to them. What's the reward for?

We are here to prove that our love is real, so guess what? Suffering is necessary, and it is actually the gate to total freedom. When are you the happiest? When you are in love and suffering doesn't feel expensive. It gives you great joy, because it brings you close to somebody. We share the fellowship of his or her sufferings, Paul says, so that somehow he can attain to the resurrection from the dead.

That's the big deal—eternal life, resurrection from the dead, salvation, getting to Heaven, paying the price, whatever it takes, choosing your value, changing your priorities, making God your source of life, rejecting anything else that competes in any way, finding out who really satisfies you. That's what life is about; evangelism, saving the lost, suffering whatever it takes. Paul said:

> *However, I consider my life worth nothing to me; my only aim is to finish the race and complete the task the Lord Jesus has given me—the task of testifying to the good news of God's grace* (Acts 20:24).

That's what brings miracles, when miracles serve God's purposes. If your heart is aligned with His, you are thrilled with Him and you are like a little kid. You don't understand anything, but you have been given grace to love, appreciate, and pour on your God the affection and sheer trust that makes Him happy—then miracles chase you and you can't help it.

You may be thinking, *Oh, Rolland, you're just being silly. There are sick people. There are people who need money. There are people with real problems. Get real!* Two years ago doctors gave me two weeks to live. My body was completely shut down. I couldn't take a shower, brush my teeth, put on my shoes, swallow, or eat. In two weeks they said my brain would completely shut down and all my bodily functions would cease. They told Heidi to call our closest friends and family to say goodbye. Believe me, when you are at a point like that, you get remarkably heavenly minded. Suddenly your priorities are clear. Jesus is all you care about, and all you want to do is pray.

Well, I hope and pray that you get that way without having to get within an inch of death. I hope and pray that you get to the point where Jesus is all you care about, and all you want to do is pray. I hope and pray that you set your priorities straight in line with God's will.

• • •

Heavenly Father, I'm so happy. I don't know why You love me so much, except that Jesus redeemed me. Thank You for loving me and for creating a relationship with me. You are all I seek—Your goodness and mercy are all I need. Lord, I pray that people will be raised from the dead physically and spiritually. May they realize that only in You can life be fully lived. In Jesus' name, amen.

Chapter 5

I WILL GET HIM

by Philip Mantofa

LET'S LOOK AT MARY MAGDALENE:

*Then the disciples went back to where they were staying. Now Mary stood outside the tomb crying. As she wept, she bent over to look into the tomb and saw two angels in white, seated where Jesus' body had been, one at the head and the other at the foot. They asked her, "Woman, why are you crying?" "They have taken my Lord away," she said, "and I don't know where they have put Him." At this, she turned around and saw Jesus standing there, but she did not realize that it was Jesus. He asked her, "Woman, why are you crying? Who is it you are looking for?" Thinking He was the gardener, she said, "Sir, if you have carried Him away, tell me where you have put Him, and **I will get Him**." Jesus said to her, "Mary." She turned toward Him and cried out in Aramaic, "Rabboni!" (which means "Teacher")* (John 20:10-16, emphasis added).

I would entitle this part of Scripture "The Furious Love of Mary Magdalene." When all the disciples went back to their homes, Mary stood outside in the cold weather, outside the tomb crying. Her love was extraordinary. When Jesus was a dead man, all the disciples said there was nothing else to gain from Him. They were saddened and felt lost—this was the end of the journey. *He's dead, what more can we get out of Him*, they thought.

Is this what the Gospel means to us? To get something out of Jesus? If that's the only Gospel we know, we are lacking much insight. Mary, an ordinary woman with an extraordinary love, was still hopelessly devoted to a dead Christ. She was someone with nothing, without any more promises. She was still devoted to Jesus Christ. She stood outside the tomb crying, and as she wept, she bent over to look into the tomb. What was she looking for? Even though there was nothing else she could expect out of Jesus, she still bent over, looking for Him. She was almost in a position of prayer and worship—a position of adoring—even though He was, she thought, a dead Christ. She bent over and looked into the tomb. She sought after Him even after death. Mary still sought Jesus even though she was hopeless.

One day satan spoke to me and I believe Jesus allowed him to speak to me just to test my faith. No—to test my love. Satan said, "You woke up one day as a preacher of the Gospel, as a teacher of God's Word. You think you know a lot of things about what the Bible says about Jesus and salvation." All of a sudden, there was much doubt in my heart. I thought, *What if Jesus isn't the way to Heaven? What if there is a god out there that I do not know that is greater than Jesus? What if I died today and when I woke up on the other side and opened my eyes, I thought I would be saved, but I was in hell? What if my belief isn't enough to get me to Heaven?*

I have to be honest, doubts do come into my heart from time to time, but love, not faith, always defeats all my doubts. Even my faith works through love. So I woke up, and I was doubting. *What if I wake up on the other side and Jesus was with me in hell?* That's a crazy thought, isn't it? But I have to be honest, I thought about it. With tears in my eyes, I answered the devil. I said, "Even if I wake up on the other side to find out that I'm in hell with Jesus, I choose to go to hell with Him...even if I cannot expect anything from Him. During my life, there has never been a god who has treated me as well as Jesus has. He has loved me. He has never once hurt me. If this Jesus I believe in is wrong, He has never treated me wrong. I'll be hopelessly devoted to Him even to hell."

That's how much I am devoted to Him. I'm not in it for any selfish gain. I'm in this faith because I love the One I believe in. I said to the devil, "Even if it turns out that the Hindu god is the right god, I won't follow that god, because I know the Hindu god has treated followers cruelly. I would never follow their gods. I will follow Jesus—period."

No Doubt

I do not doubt that Jesus is the only way to Heaven. And I'm not saying this ignorantly. Many years ago, God took my spirit to hell. I saw what hell was really like, and I would be so afraid of going there. I'm absolutely convinced that if I did not have Jesus, I would certainly end up there. This dear, distraught Mary was standing outside in the cold weather that day—she chose Jesus. Mary's devotion to a dead Christ is more devotion than our devotion to the living Christ today. I have chosen Mary's kind of faith, not the kind of faith I see in the majority of Christians today. Many are in it for something. They want to get something out of Christ, but I have fallen in love with Him and nothing can take away this love.

Has what I said disturbed you somehow? I'm not teaching you to doubt Christ—I believe Christ is the only way, the truth, and the life. I don't believe in pluralism. I don't believe that all roads lead to Rome. Yes, maybe Rome, but not to Heaven, no way. All I'm trying to do is to teach you to love Christ unconditionally as He has loved you.

The morning satan spoke to me was one of real spiritual warfare. I had to defeat satan completely. I said to him, "Yes, if Jesus goes to hell, I go with Him—get lost, satan. You can't steal my faith. My faith cannot be stolen because my faith is not belief; my faith is love. It's greater than just believing. Maybe you can take my belief for a few seconds this morning, but I'm still sticking with Jesus because of my love for Him."

And [Mary] *saw two angels in white, seated where Jesus' body had been, one at the head and the other at the foot* (John 20:12).

When I read this verse, I realized that Mary wasn't a stupid person. She was there from early in the morning. She had seen no one around, and when she entered the tomb, it was empty and she saw two angels. The Bible says she knowingly saw two angels, not two men. She knew she saw angels, and I am impressed at how *unimpressed* Mary was at seeing angels. When most people nowadays see angels, they brag about it to impress everyone. God uses some people to heal the sick once, and they run around bragging how great they are.

I don't want to build my faith and my ministry upon performance, not even upon miracles. No, my relationship with Christ is purely love and a furious kind if necessary. Not furious at Him, but furious to those who take Jesus for granted. I love America, but I'm going to take you on for not appreciating Jesus.

Wherever I preach in the world, I'm ready to die there. In Indonesia, where I'm from, I've preached in places where I received death threats. I spoke on a certain island once where my life was threatened, and some people hired two bodyguards for me. They had guns and training. One day I said, "Please sirs, tomorrow don't bring your guns anymore. Actually, my life is not in your hands but your lives are now in mine." So at the end of the crusade, I got to pray for these men to surrender their lives to Christ. I'm willing to lay down my life when I preach. And when I come to America, I'm ready to die here. I'm willing to make myself hated by everyone if that can make someone love Christ a little bit more.

Mary saw two angels and she wasn't even stunned. She didn't even talk about it. Her focus was solely on Jesus. Unfortunately, much of the gospel that goes around the world right now, especially in the Western countries, is the gospel of angels—not the Gospel of Christ. And when pastors preach only the prosperity gospel, they have robbed the Gospel of its prosperity. I have seen more people line up to get blessed than to get persecuted. That's how I know they are believing in the gospel of angels, not Christ.

One day in 1998, I was at a certain place in Indonesia when all hell broke loose. I was serving a congregation in a certain part of Java Island where I come from, and it was near one of the fiercest riots. All the Muslims were on the streets and I was in the church praying with a number of pastors and seminary students—everybody was scared, including me. I thought, *Oh gosh, no, no. At least, God, allow me to get married first.* Everyone was praying, "Dear God, please save us! Please save us! Danger is near." You could hear the drums getting nearer and nearer to the church as it was on the main street. From the reports of what had already happened elsewhere, we thought for sure the

IGNITING *furious* LOVE

church would be burned down and the women would be raped before we would all be murdered. We were praying and praying, "Dear Jesus, please save us."

Jesus, rebuked me lovingly, "Please, don't be so over confident. So many people have asked Me, petitioned Me that they can be My martyrs. Don't be so deceived, for your blood may not be holy enough to be sacrificed on My altar. Your proposal can get rejected, so what are you afraid of?" It's almost like I was saying, "Oh Jesus, please don't let me be the president of the United States." Who says Jesus would make me one? It's almost like you would come to me and say, "Philip, please, please don't give me money." I said I won't. What makes you think I would give you money? Please don't give me your house, your car. Who says I would? To ask to be persecuted in His name is like asking for great wishes. He saved us that day, but there were many other Christians who died. Now I was no longer overjoyed by the fact that we just narrowly escaped death, because I had missed my chance to lay down my life for His name.

Mary, too, wasn't amazed at the two angels in the tomb. Miracles are nothing. Power, wealth, blessings are no big deal. Love is the greatest!

The angels asked her, *"Woman, why are you crying?"* (John 20:13). Mary didn't say, "Oh my gosh, you're angels! Can I get your autograph?" No, that didn't happen. She said, *"They have taken my Lord away, and I don't know where they have put Him."* She chose His presence over the gift of seeing and conversing with angels and experiencing the supernatural. She was so preoccupied with the presence of Jesus, who was now absent. She asked, "Where is my Lord?"

• 100 •

Prayer, Miracles, and Reading the Word

I am so sad that many Christians don't seek His presence. It's not about how many hours you pray; it's about the desire. Go back to the basics. He won't force us to fellowship with Him. He does not need to speak audibly to me to get me to kneel and pray. The Lord knows that my heart is always directed toward Him in love; and at the gentlest flow of His power, without even asking, I immediately kneel.

Building an intimate and serious relationship with the Lord is so important that I would not exchange five minutes of my time with Him for five hours of power flowing through me in which people are resurrected from the dead. Many miracles happen in my ministry without me always realizing, sometimes even when I'm not talking about them, and then miracles pop up here and there; but when I focus on just the miracles, not much happens.

Actually, I would choose both if I could. I would choose spending time with the Lord *and* seeing miracles as well. However, if I had to choose between personal time with Him and time accomplishing His mighty works before men, I would definitely choose five minutes with the One I love. Still, I believe that God will use those who are intimate with Him in most extraordinary ways—including the dead being raised to life.

Therefore, don't try to attract people to church by saying that miracles happen and that they will be touched if they attend. No, just tell them who Jesus is to you. Then live out that faith. That's all it takes and you will see revival like never before.

"They have taken my Lord away," she said, "and I don't know where they have put Him." At this, she turned around and saw Jesus standing there, but she didn't realize that it was

Jesus. He asked her, "Woman, why are you crying? Who is it you are looking for?" Thinking He was the gardener, she said, "Sir, if you have carried Him away, tell me where you have put Him, and I will get Him" (John 20:13-16).

Listen up, America, tell me, where have you laid my Savior in your life? Have you taken my Lord away? Tell me, have you taken Him for granted? Do you still pray a prayer of thanks before meals at school and work? At home, I must confess that sometimes I'll forget to pray before meals, because I have such a relaxed relationship with Jesus. It's not like I will choke if I don't pray before my meal, but I make it a point when I am in public to bow my head and pray. I thank Him and show people around me that I know who provides the food I eat to nourish my body. If you are ashamed of doing that, especially young people, give Jesus to me. I'll take Him for my people in Indonesia. And I'll make sure that every time we bow our heads before meals in schools and on campuses, our young people will pray twice as long, so much longer for you, just for you.

Indonesia has taken the crumbs of the American gospel, just the crumbs, and we have become a strong group of Christians. We are only enjoying the leftovers, not even the bread. You have enjoyed the bread, but what have you done with it? I don't want to offend you. I say what I say with love—to help you understand how very privileged you are in the United States. But some of you have not given to the poor. You are not giving to the lost; instead, you have made yourself bread factories for business sake. God doesn't need factories. God needs people with obedient hands and feet, people who profess and teach not just the gospel of the angels or prosperity.

When I preach, there are manifestations and hundreds of thousands of people receive Christ just by the crumbs. In the beginning, I didn't have high expectations for my nation. People kept telling me that it was impossible to preach the Gospel in Indonesia—the largest Muslim-populated country in the world. But I preached anyway with a hopeless devotion to perishing souls. I was hopeful for the crumbs from the Master's table. Today, when I preach, supernatural manifestations happen and hundreds of thousands of people receive Christ just by those crumbs. Now don't be flattered by the bread—it does no good if the focus of the heart isn't right. We use your crumbs, and people of all faiths in Indonesia and across Asia are turning to Jesus as their Savior in an unprecedented way.

Envies Intensely

Or do you think Scripture says without reason that He jealously longs [envies intensely] *for the Spirit He has caused to dwell in us?* (James 4:5)

In describing the Holy Spirit, James 4:5 can also be interpreted as, "Or do you think Scripture says without reason that the Spirit He caused to live in us envies intensely?" I'm not good at describing the Holy Spirit in theological terms, even though I know how. I've been to seminary for four years. But I can explain the Holy Spirit with the language of my heart.

Acts 1:8 says, *"But you will receive power when the Holy Spirit comes on you; and you will be my witnesses to Me in Jerusalem, and in all Judea and Samaria, and to the end of the earth."* It is clear that when you receive the Holy Spirit, you receive power and will be witnesses to the ends of the earth. This is a very important verse. But there is an equally important verse prior that we often neglect, *"On one occasion, while He was eating with them, He gave them this command: 'Do not leave Jerusalem, but wait for the gift My Father promised, which you have heard Me speak about"* (Acts 1:4). Jesus was telling them to remain in the city until they received the promise of the Father—the Holy Spirit is the promise of the Father.

I have three children and I love them all so deeply. My eldest is a daughter, Vanessa, and I love her very much. I view Vanessa as precious as the Holy Spirit is to the Father. The illustration I have chosen to describe the Holy Spirit relationship to the Father God is a lame illustration compared to the real thing, but I love my daughter so much I would give anything to her. I love Vanessa so, so much that I am willing to die for her every day.

If one day she marries a man and that man abuses her, I will not accept that. If Vanessa has a boyfriend someday and that boyfriend crosses the line in terms of holiness, he will face the dragon in me. I have prayed for my children's spouses since they were born. I fast for their spouses. I will be very careful in helping my daughter choose her soul mate but if I give my daughter to a young man to be his, and he is not appreciative of her—at any time, I will welcome that young man to return her to me. I will love her for him. Got it?

That's what I believe it means that the Holy Spirit envies intensely, that He jealously longs. The Father envies intensely. Have you, today, treated the Holy Spirit well? Has He found a good dwelling place in your life? We must love the Holy Spirit at least the same as the Father loves Him. Don't get into a debate about the Trinity. I believe that we must love Him; we must desire Him at least like His Father does, at least the same if not more.

Intimacy with Him

My friend, how do you treat the Holy Spirit? Do you honor the Holy Spirit in your life by living in holiness? When you address a judge you say, "Your Honor." If you were to meet a king or queen, you say, "Your highness." When you speak to the Holy Spirit, it is appropriate to say, "Your Holiness, speak, I'm here to listen to You." You are honoring Him. If you want to honor Him in your life, then live every day in His holiness.

Christianity isn't about being different in the sense that we are crazy. It is about being evident, evidently holy. The evidence is the most important of all. It's not our styles of worship. It's not about that. It's about how we can obviously show that we live holy lives in honor of the Holy Spirit.

To walk in intimacy with Him, we have to honor the person of the Holy Spirit, and we have to honor the Holy Bible. We can't walk in intimacy with God if we don't honor the Bible. Even in these days of high technology, I still like to use my old Bible. Some people have their Bible in their iPhone or Blackberry. But I still like my old-fashioned Bible where I can write down notes and thoughts. God has taught me that if I cannot love the physical Bible, I cannot love the Word of God in it. Bibles, whether paper or electronic, are not God—but a Bible contains the Word of God.

While I was still in Bible school, I went to a certain village in Indonesia for field education during summer vacation. To receive credit for field education, I was to serve with the local people. One day I saw this older lady who was dressed nicely, carrying a big Bible into church. Church services had just concluded when it began to rain heavily. I thought the lady would use her Bible to cover her beautiful hair. No, rather she covered the Bible so it wouldn't get wet. She was soaked, but the Bible was dry. I thought, *Wow, that's my hero of faith.* Nameless, faceless as she was, she was my hero.

I want to be such a Christian. I love my Bible with all my heart—but I don't worship the Bible. I worship the God of the

Bible. I have a personal relationship with my Bible. There is no magic in the Book or the material that made it, but every time I touch my Bible, I receive a revelation. There is no substitute for the Holy Bible. None.

If you want to walk in intimacy with God, then honor the Bible. Read it and do it. It's as simple as that. Consider this your lifetime homework. I don't read the Bible with my brain only, I also read the Bible with my heart—and with prayers between verses, which makes reading the Bible a very personal interaction with my heavenly Father. I'll give you an example:

Blessed are they whose ways are blameless, who walk according to the law of the Lord. Blessed are they who keep His statutes and seek Him with all their heart—they do no wrong but follow His ways. You have laid down precepts that are to be fully obeyed. Oh, that my ways were steadfast in obeying Your decrees! (Psalm 119:1-5)

All I want is You, Lord. You know it. If I could please You in walking in holiness, I would be satisfied. You can take anything else and I would be fine.

Then I would not be put to shame when I consider all Your commands. I will praise You with an upright heart as I learn your righteous laws (Psalm 119:6-7).

Please see my heart. Oh, I dream. This is my greatest dream in my life. It is not to be famous, not to be liked by others, but that I could cry out to You from an upright heart. I don't think my heart is quite upright yet, Lord, but as I learn Your righteous laws, I will obey Your decrees. Do not ever forsake me. Take anything in my life, but do not take the Holy Spirit from me; cast me not away from Your presence. Take not thy Holy Spirit from me.

How can a young person stay on the path of purity? By living according to your word (Psalm 119:9).

Use me while I'm still in my youth, Lord. Remember not the sins of my youth. Use me while I am still young. Then I will know that I have given You the best part of my life. Use me now. I'm not getting younger day by day, month by month, or year by year. I want to give You the best. I want to serve You now.

I seek you with all of my heart; do not let me stray from your commands (Psalm 119:10).

Praise be to You, Lord; teach me Your decrees. With my lips I recount all the laws that come from Your mouth. I rejoice in following Your statutes as one rejoices in great riches (Psalm 119:12-14).

You are my only wealth in life. O God, when I forget that, please forgive me. In any second of my life when I'm forgetting that, please forgive me. Please forgive Your son, I pray.

I meditate on your precepts and consider your ways (Psalm 119:15).

I have just let you in on my private conversation with my Lord—when it's just Him and me. I have had this intimate relationship with Him from 1992, since the first time I met Him—the first time He found me. Our relationship has never changed. I read ten chapters a day, at least.

The Bible and Spiritual Books

I studied theology at Columbia Bible College in Vancouver, Canada, but was thirsty for more knowledge about the things of the Lord. I was young, naïve, and gullible, and the believers around me seemed very knowledgeable. After returning to

Indonesia from Canada, I had occasion to observe the world of Christianity in Indonesia. At that time, reading spiritual books was the trend among Indonesian Christians and many deemed them helpful to their spiritual growth.

I felt out of step with my peers, preachers, and especially the youth my age who were satisfying their thirst for knowledge by diligently reading spiritual books. There was only one Book in my life. Aside from reading requirements for seminary, I only wanted to read the Bible.

At times it seemed that Christians revered spiritual books more than their Bibles. The Bible wasn't real for them. They saw it as an outdated textbook. When I talked to them about Scriptures, they seemed uninterested. One day I prayed, "Lord, You know I love You and I love Your Word. You know that right now this Bible is the one and only Book in my life. But Lord, allow me for the next year, only for the next year, to draw knowledge from spiritual books. I feel out of place with my peers, especially young servants of the Lord. They seem to be getting spiritual knowledge from these other books…from these spiritual books. I don't own even one, but my friends have so many. I won't get anywhere if just kept reading Genesis to Revelation all the time. Haven't I already read this Bible from cover to cover?"

Actually I have lost count how many times I've repeated reading the Bible from Genesis to Revelation.

"Lord, allow me not to read the Bible just for one year; during that year, I will study all the good spiritual books that people say can bring me closer to You and help me be used by God in extraordinary ways."

The Lord didn't answer me, but I badgered Him with that prayer.

"Just one year, Lord. After that I will return to my former relationship with my Bible. I'll use that year as a break from the Bible. We all need a break. I don't want the others to leave me behind." After I said amen, I forsook my Bible and locked it in my desk drawer.

The next day, a miracle happened.

The following day, I wanted to get something I had left in my Bible. When I picked up the Bible from the drawer and opened the cover, I was amazed—my Bible was wet, soaked with oil. The oil saturated my Bible, filling the air with fragrance. *Who spilled oil on my Bible,* I wondered. I thought *someone had spilled some of the anointing oil that I carried everywhere in those days.* But it had been a long time since I carried any oil. Then where did this oil come from?

I was perplexed, especially because the drawer had been locked. I tried wiping the oil off my pants, but they were ruined because the oil stain wouldn't come out. Finally, with much effort, I succeeded in wiping up the oil until the Bible was dry. It was a little wet but not as much as when I first found it. Then I returned my Bible to the drawer and locked it again.

The next day curiosity compelled me to check the Bible again. I really wanted to know who had spilled oil on my Bible. I unlocked the drawer and opened the Bible. It was saturated with oil just like the day before, soaking wet and sticky. I wasn't brave enough to open it again. But suddenly, I felt a great anointing and presence in the room. With a trembling voice, I asked Him, "Why did that happen, Lord? What do You want to tell me?" I wiped the oil from my Bible and put it on a table. Its fragrance filled the room.

Still trembling, I knelt at the Lord's feet, "What is Your message behind this?" I knew the Lord never did anything without a purpose. It was vital that I learn what it was. That day, the Holy Spirit clearly spoke to my heart. "Philip, do you want to be close to God?" he asked. "Do you want Me to use you? Do you want to become an anointed man of God?" Holy Spirit asked.

I believe that an experience like that will not happen to other spiritual books, but only through the old-fashioned Bible. The Lord opened my eyes, and I realized my decision to leave the Bible for one year for the sake of reading other spiritual books was wrong. Anointing comes only from the Bible.

The Lord showed me that if I wanted to be anointed by God, stay close to Him, and be used by Him, I must meditate on His Word day and night and do whatever is written in it. After the Lord opened my eyes, I realized that the others were the ones who were out of step with God, not me. Reading and putting into practice God's written Word is the way we develop an intimate relationship with Christ. The highest authority is still God's Word—not our experiences, no matter how spectacular, and not other spiritual books.

He reprimanded me. He became jealous because my intimacy with the Bible was threatened when I began to care about other people's opinions and spiritual books. Jesus was jealous, intensely jealous. The Lord was so happy to see me draw close to Him through His Word that He prepared a miracle that prevented me from taking the wrong path and brought me back to the truth. He sent that miracle so I would never be far from my Bible—just like that lady in that small town during the rain shower.

When the Holy Spirit revealed this to me, I wept and firmly took hold of my Bible again. Obviously the Lord liked the way I read His Word, and He didn't want me to stop. He sent a miracle just to make sure I wouldn't forsake it.

I believe God was telling me that He poured water from a stone for the sake of making Himself known to the Israelites. On that day, to make me understand, He poured oil from my Bible so I would know that no other book is anointed like the Bible, which contains His written Word. The Book is truth for those who believe and lay hold of it. After the Lord revealed this truth to me, the oil stopped flowing. A month after the oil ceased, my Bible peeled apart from the front to the back cover. First I hid away that Bible so people wouldn't worship it. Then I destroyed it because of this.

Today when I have time, I read spiritual books as supplemental reading. For others, spiritual books are the primary reading material and the Bible is the supplement. Some people interpret the Bible through the other books they read; but for me, the Bible is the lens through which I read the other books. The Lord built my ministry on the foundation of the truth of God's Word. The foundation of my life is this written Word, and the revelations I receive come purely from God's Word. My foundation is firm.

Love the Bible, please. I beg you. The Holy Spirit that is in us envies intensely. Do you love the Holy Spirit? Then live a holy life. Do you want to be intimate with the Holy Spirit? Then read the Bible. It's simple. Grab your Bible, hold it tightly, read it and do it; you will be blessed.

• • •

O Lord, You found us when we were still unworthy. We desire You more than anything. You know our hearts and we love You more than anyone in our lives. All we want in this life, Lord, is to know You. That's all. Our souls are consumed with longing for Your laws at all times. You rebuke the arrogant, who are cursed and who stray from Your commands. Remove from us scorn and contempt, for we will keep Your statutes. Lord, do not let us be put to shame. Even if the whole world goes the wrong way, give us the grace to still follow You. If we be alone in the world following You, we will do that. You have set our hearts free to love You. Let us have the devotion of Mary who sought You in the tomb.

Chapter 6

SIMPLY LOVE

by Shampa Rice

FIRST CORINTHIANS 13:1, *"IF I speak in the tongues of men or of angels, but do not have love, I am only a resounding gong or a clanging symbol."*

I can know the tongues of angels, but even so, in the eyes of Heaven, if I do not have love, I am simply a big, ugly noise. And though I have the gift of prophecy and can understand all mysteries and all knowledge—in other words, even if I was like Elijah, and understood all mysteries even if I was like Daniel, and had all wisdom like Solomon, and could move mountains with so much faith like Moses—I have impressed nobody, maybe people, but not Heaven.

Heaven is unimpressed if we do not have love. We are simply nothing. And though we bestow all goods to the poor as a display of our godliness, as did Mother Teresa, if we do it without love, it is worthless.

I grew up across the street from where Mother Teresa ministered in India. All my life I watched this woman. When I was little, my friends and I would run across the street and grab and hug her legs; and I remember looking at her feet. She had large, pancake-sized feet. As children do, we laughed at her feet. And she would just smile. Forever she was wrinkled; there was never a time when she was not wrinkled. So all my life, she was the same to me; she didn't change.

Mother Teresa never wore shoes or sandals; she walked with bare feet. We wanted to copy her, so we also didn't wear shoes, until our parents put an end to that. But I really wanted to be like her. I wanted to go and join her order. I was planning on running away. When you join the order of sisters, once you go inside their compound, nobody can really get you out. If you sign your name—it doesn't matter if you are only 13—you are in. Your parents have nothing to do with it; they really cannot take you out.

So I planned to do that, because I really wanted to help Mother Teresa in her work. But I had a mom who was all seeing and all knowing. God told her about my plan. She didn't scold me. She just came quietly and said, "You know, Shampa, you don't have to run away in order to answer the call of God on your life."

I looked at her and said, "I really want to be like her."

"Shampa, I know that. I know your heart, but you don't understand. You have something...something a bit different from Mother Teresa. God will help you do what she does. But you see, Sweetheart, as you walk with Christ, Christ will show you—where she left off, you can pick up."

What we learn to love, we will leave behind for others to learn to love. We must embrace and pursue love like Paul describes in First Corinthians 13. We will have to make a conscious effort to pursue love. Let's pursue love, shall we? Let's pursue love more than you and I could ever dream of pursuing anything else. I read that the most common thread running through all the greatest revivals worldwide is the simplicity of God's love. Christ loves us, and we are to love others—it's that simple.

Unfortunately, many have been raised in homes and schools that put stipulations on love: if I do this and that, then I will be loved; or, I didn't do that and this so that's why they don't love me. We have been raised holding a little flower in our hand and tearing off the petals while singing, "She loves me, she loves me not...he loves me, he loves me not."

But today, you can hold a flower and say, "Christ loves me, Christ loves me, Christ loves me, Christ loves me, Christ loves me"...and in the end it's still, "Christ loves me!" Allow Christ's love to seep into the deepest part of your being—soul, spirit, mind, and body. That's the true and simple confidence that will keep you from being afraid.

What kind of person can be dragged through the jungles half the night on his bare back, be left for dead, and awakened by birds singing, only to stand up, be surprised that he's standing, see blood on the ground but not on his body, and walk back to his hut? This happened to one of my sons, Josiah. What caused him to be unharmed? What caused the wild animals not to eat him up? What caused him to stand up and hear the birds, and find on his body not a single mark? What is it? Don't you think it's the love of God? That's how great His love is for little people. His love is what keeps these people going right back over and over again to where they were beaten, threatened, and violated. They want to show His love to those who have no hope without Him.

What Is This Love?

What is this love? Why is it so strange and so ridiculous that a human being loses common sense? They know they may get killed, but they return again to dangerous areas. No, they are not praying that the persecution will stop, because they know from Acts 2 that the disciples did not pray for the persecution to stop. When Peter was caught with John, what did he do? He went back and they released him, the high priest, and all of them. They gathered together and then they released him because they couldn't find any fault; and they said, "If you do it again, we will beat you." And Peter and John said, "Well, either we obey you or obey God. And they walked away."

When they went back to their friends who were praying and shared everything that happened, what was it that came out of their mouths? They lifted their voices to Heaven! "God! Give us wisdom and strength. Give us boldness to stand before them." They did *not* pray, "God, stop the persecution." If the persecution didn't come, the Church would have died many thousands of years ago. It would not have reached us. The love of God would not have been preached.

Do you work out and keep your body in shape? Why do you work out? Why would you want to persecute your body? Think about it: the P90X workout schedule is grueling. Why would you want to do it? It hurts! Are you crazy? Why? Because you know you are going to get in shape, so much so that you can hike or bike or run and not grow weary; you can stomp up any mountain. You can climb, and you will not be tired; you can walk, and you will not faint.

If you can do that in your body, how much more does your spirit need to be worked on? So how do you work on your spirit? Well, I ask, beg, and get desperate—I will not do anything until

God fills me with His love. That's what happened to me nine years ago when I found out that it's worthless to preach the Gospel, simply worthless, without the love of God.

So here I was at a conference in the Punjab with hundreds and hundreds of women sitting there, and I was doing what Christ told me, "Shampa, you will speak nothing."

"But Lord, it's a conference; they've all come to hear me. How do I go about this, Lord? I mean, it's going to be really, really silly if I say I have nothing to share."

So Christ said, "No, no, no. You are going to have them make a line and then tell them that all you are going to do is hug them."

I said, "Oh, well that's easy; that's a good one." You just hug people; it's so wonderful. As I stood there and hugged hundreds and hundreds of ladies, one after the other, they would fall on the ground and weep their guts out and start sharing things. They shared about their abuse at home; they shared about the trauma they go through. And as I'm hearing it, I couldn't handle it. I thought I was going to go crazy, and I knew that I didn't have what it took. I knew that; I knew I was not prepared for that kind of sorrow and trauma that they were going through.

So by the time we were done with the hugging, it was two in the morning, and I looked at the translator, the pastor's wife, and said, "I have to go to my room. I'm feeling really sick," which I was. I was feeling so sick in my heart. And I said, "Would you kindly continue," and she said yes. So I ran to my room, locked the door, and screamed at God, "You have to do something inside of me. I don't have what it takes! Did you hear them tonight? Did you hear their stories? I can't handle it," I said, "I'm limited. I do not know how to hear them and keep sane in my head. I feel like I'm going crazy."

And I told God, "You've got to do something inside of me; there's a lack. I don't have something and I don't know what it is. I don't know what I'm lacking, but I know I don't have it. So whatever it is, You have to give it to me; and if You don't give it to me, I'm going to stay in this room. I'm not going out. I'm not going to sleep; I'm just going to keep standing here screaming at You."

God in a Headlock

It was like getting God in a headlock. Try it sometime. It works; it's great. So I continued to scream at God, "Look! Those ladies are crying out to You. They're not crying out to me, because they know I don't have the answer. I know You love them, so give it to me, whatever it is." All of a sudden the wall became a huge screen, and in this screen was a tiny heart. And then this big hand came with a big, big jug. Inside the jug was a pinkish color liquid.

And then the voice of the Lord came, "Shampa, watch what I do." *Wow, this is incredible,* I thought. Then the jug started pouring the liquid into the tiny heart, and the heart got bigger and bigger and bigger. Even though more of this liquid was being poured in, the little heart did not burst. It simply made room. "This is incredible. It's like a balloon, isn't it?" I asked.

He said, "No, it's not, Shampa, it's not a balloon...it's your heart."

I said, "Oh, and what is it You're pouring?"

"It's My love—that's enough. If you never preach one more time," God said, "if you never ever share one more time, or if you never see the blind eyes open one more time, and you never see the dead being raised, and you never do any deliverances ever again—but if you have My love in your heart, Shampa, that is enough. That's all I care about, for My people to beg Me for My love and nothing else. You would do enough. That's all you need."

I fell on my face. I didn't know when I fell asleep or what time it was, but I got up in the morning, ran downstairs, and I have been going downstairs ever since. God keeps me from getting overwhelmed. He said, "You just keep begging Me, Shampa, and I'll keep filling you up, and you will be able to handle it every single time. You will never feel like you're losing it."

I said, "All right, I trust You, Lord." So He has been giving us children. Lots and lots of kids are at risk in India. About 300 girls every month are being sold to temples, Hindu temples. In one tiny district alone, 300 young girls are being exploited as temple prostitutes or sacrificed before the goddess. Children as young as 4 years of age are being horribly abused.[1]

What can rescue them if not God's great love; anything less will not be able to keep them. Yeah, you can rescue them, and that's fine. Then what? Will they be better off? We have to have His love in order to make a difference; otherwise, don't rescue them. They can only have a better life if the love of God is involved, otherwise there is no better life.

During World War II, a Russian dissident made a negative comment about Stalin. Alexander Solzhenitsyn was promptly thrown into exile. While in exile, he wasn't just sitting around feeling sorry for himself. He wrote plays and poetry, which still influence churches around the world. He made this statement:

> If only it were all so simple! If only there were evil people somewhere insidiously committing evil deeds, and it were necessary only to separate them from the

rest of us and destroy them. But the line dividing good and evil cuts through the heart of every human being. And who is willing to destroy a piece of his own heart?[2]

Who is willing? You and I cannot judge the people who are hurting and harming innocent little children. That's what Christ speaks to me, over and over again: "Shampa, you would do the exact same thing, or even worse if it wasn't for My love that you recognize and accept. That's the grace that you have."

I am no better than those people. We all have very, very wicked hearts. But when our hearts are given to this great love of God, all of a sudden everything shifts and then we see the way Christ sees, and we love the way Christ loves. And when we hurt the way He hurts, we run to Him for a hug, because we don't know anything else. May we pursue His love. May we not do anything less than that. The way we live ought to manifest what we believe. The way we live ought to manifest the truth of what we believe. So let's live and love. Thank You, sweet Jesus.

His Great Love

I would like to impress Christ with everything inside of me. Even unconsciously, I want Him to be impressed. How can I do that? I pursue His love and it's enough. It's enough, because out of that flows everything. God will not hold back when you please His heart. He just simply cannot. So even if you are not the least bit aware of miracles taking place, they are. We have all sorts of crazy things happening. For instance, there was a man people called the "pretzel man" because his arms and legs were all curled up. When I returned to the area where he lived after having a conference there previously, I asked about the pretzel man. How is he doing? Is he still alive? I was told, "The last time you came and you hugged him, he got up the next morning and was perfectly fine!" He had missed three years of work because his arms and legs were all curled up. But because of the love of God, he is healed.

The love of God is like that. It is effortless. So you and I don't have to put any effort into it—in fact, I believe that He doesn't want us to. It is supposed to be effortless. It is not supposed to be so much work that we have to conjure up some kind of power within us. It's supposed to simply happen. Why? Because you and I are filled with His love. And His love wants to heal; His love wants to patch people in the deepest part of their spirit. His love wants to go deeper in their soul, where they are hurt, wounded, disappointed, and betrayed. His love would like to do that. So all you and I have to do is be filled with His love. And then we become the devil's worse nightmare!

You don't have to be a certain something, a certain name that everybody knows. You can be a little, but powerful person. That's why I'm just a teapot; I even wear a little teapot necklace, that's who I am. I'm from the kitchen, and most kitchens have one teapot sitting on the stove. You don't go to your friend's house and say, "Wow! You have a teapot!" You are not at all surprised to see a teapot on the stove. But when your friend says, "Hey, come on in, would you like some tea?" You immediately say, "I would love some." And then you sit in a little chair at a little table and have a cup of tea and feel so loved and welcomed and accepted. You and I are little teapots. We get filled with love and simply pour out. That's what teapots are made for, to pour a hot cup of tea.

Be filled with His love to overflowing and desire love as well as pursue it. I know, I know. Many want to see the dead raised, to see angels, to be healed—I know that. But you can train your mind and your spirit to desire love and this gives you understanding for all the rest. That's what I do. I want to desire

His love so much that I become like what is described in the following hymn. These lines were scribbled on the wall of an insane asylum in 1917 in England. They were so beautiful that Fredrick Lehman made a hymn out of them:

> "Could we with ink, the ocean fill, and were the skies of parchment made, were every stalk on earth a quill and every man a scribe by trade. To write the love of God above, will drain the ocean dry. Nor could the scroll contain the whole, though stretched from sky to sky."

Was this written by an insane man? Perhaps not. And even if that was the case, I would chose insanity rather than live without knowing His Great love. I would rather be in an insane asylum than not experience His great love.

His great love is the only answer to every man and woman's need. I could write for years sharing with you miracles after miracles that the Lord has done by His great love. That would make you feel very good, very lifted up, but that's not my goal. My goal is for you to be mesmerized by His great love so much so that from right now there will be a deep shift within you, that you would become the quill in God's hand so He can write His great love on people's hearts. I pray that you and I would be so pliable and so easy in the hand of the Lord that people will see Him through us.

I was 16 years of age when I found a flower in a beautiful garden in India and every little petal was one of the seven colors of the rainbow. I started weeping, holding the flower gently in my hand. I wept my guts out and asked, "What must it have taken You…how much time You must have spent on this flower? Why would You do that for just one flower? Why didn't You make it all white, all red, or all pink? Why would You spend so much time painting every petal giving it all the colors of the rainbow? What was it that caused You to do that?"

And the Lord very softly said, "Shampa, that flower was so still in My hand that it was very easy for Me to paint all the colors of Heaven on this one flower. Would you be still in My hand?"

Let us be still so He can paint the colors of love inside and outside; we don't even have to say a word. For example, I was in Wal-Mart one time looking at some clothes and this lady came toward me wearing a shirt that said "How May I Help You?"

"Oh, no, ma'am. I'm fine. I don't need help," I told her when she asked.

But she said, "I do."

"You do?" I asked.

"Yes, do you have a Bible?" she said.

Wow, I was surprised. I don't look like a church lady; I wasn't wearing a shirt that read "God Loves You," nothing like that. I said, "Why would you need a Bible?"

"I just got to get back to God," she said.

"You do? Now why would you need to get back to God?" I said. It is always good to ask questions. Many people are very eager to tell you things you need to know to help them.

"Well, I have not been walking with the Lord," she said.

"Why would you all of a sudden be stirred up to walk with God?" I asked.

"I don't know," she said.

I said, "Good, then you and I can both learn to walk with God, shall we?" So I held her, hugged her, and we started praying and weeping. This other lady came over to us. She was also wearing a "How May I Help You?" shirt. She asked if we are OK. I asked if she was getting stirred to walk with God too.

"I don't have a clue what you're talking about," she said. But very soon the three of us were weeping.

We don't need to wear a "God Loves You" shirt. You and I need to make the statement ourselves. Not just an occasional "God bless you." Many of us are so afraid to say "I love you" to strangers; we would rather play it safe and say "God bless you." Why? This one young man actually told me, "You're the first one to tell me 'I love you.' You Christians are afraid to say 'I love you.' You always say 'God loves you,' because you don't, and you want to play it safe and say 'God loves you.' But when you're standing in front of me, how will I believe God loves me. You're the one in front of me, but why should I believe you when you can't tell me you love me?"

There's truth there, right? Let's wear love, shall we? Let's become the message; we are the message. You don't have to scream loudly. You don't have to yell. You don't have to do anything to draw attention. His love will draw attention wherever you go. No matter where you are, it doesn't matter. You can be in a plane, in a train, in school; you can be taking a walk.

Carry My Love

God knows us better than anyone else. He tells us, "All you need to do is carry My love. It is as simple as that. You just simply ask Me to fill you up to overflowing, so that wherever you are—even if you don't want to minister, don't want to do anything, you don't even feel like it—I will overrule all that with

My great love. Why? Because I love My people more than you will ever know. I love My people, and I want to reach out to them with My great love. And I will do it My way; you simply be filled with My love and watch what comes next. You never have to overdo anything. My love will overdo. If you overdo, you will retard My plan."

And aren't we wonderful at retarding God's plan? Yes, we just totally mess it up sometimes. He has a way of doing things and we think we need help. Let's look at John 6:1-10:

> *Some time after this, Jesus crossed to the far shore of the Sea of Galilee (that is, the Sea of Tiberias), and a great crowd of people followed Him because they saw the signs He had performed by healing the sick. Then Jesus went up on a mountainside and sat down with His disciples. The Jewish Passover Festival was near. When Jesus looked up and saw a great crowd coming toward Him, He said to Philip, "Where shall we buy bread for these people to eat?" He asked this only to test him, for He already had in mind what He was going to do. Philip answered him, "It would take more than half a year's wages to buy enough bread for each one to have a bite!" Another of His disciples, Andrew, Simon Peter's brother, spoke up, "Here is a boy with five small barley loaves and two small fish, but how far will they go among so many?" Jesus said, "Have the people sit down." There was plenty of grass in that place, and they sat down (about five thousand men were there).*

So Jesus saw a sea of many, many people. He turned to one of the disciples, Philip, and said, "Where shall we find bread? Where can we buy enough to feed all these people?" But of course Jesus knew what He was going to do. Philip said 200 denarii worth of bread was not sufficient for them. Not even a little piece. And then Andrew told them that there was a little chap with five loafs, and two small fishes. Poor Andrew, he should have stopped right there, but he wondered how that small amount could feed so many. Jesus had everybody sit down. About five thousand men sat down on the grass—along with their families. There were none less than eight or nine thousand people, including women and children.

> *Jesus then took the loaves, gave thanks, and distributed to those who were seated as much as they wanted. He did the same with the fish. When they had all had enough to eat, He said to His disciples, "Gather the pieces that are left over. Let nothing be wasted." So they gathered them and filled twelve baskets with the pieces of the five barley loaves left over by those who had eaten. After the people saw the sign Jesus performed, they began to say, "Surely this is the Prophet who is to come into the world"* (John 6:11-14).

Jesus took the two loaves of bread and gave thanks. Then He gave it to the disciples who distributed it to the people. When they were all fed, He told His disciples to gather the fragments so that nothing would go to waste. They gathered 12 baskets full of all the bread and the fish left over.

This is one of my favorite stories in the Bible. Do you know why? It's that little boy who brought his lunch; let's look at it from the little boy's perspective. He gets up in the morning, and he tells his mom, "Mom, today I'm going to see that crazy man. You know, the One who does all those miracles. He loves kids. OK?

And his mother asks, "You'll be safe?"

"Yes, Mom, I will be safe. Just give me some good lunch. Yes!"

The mom goes into her little kitchen and makes some bread. The little boy peeps in, and sees her, *Oh, I just love my mom,* he thinks, *look at her making me lunch to take along to see Jesus.* And the mom happily sings while making five loaves of bread and gives it to him in a little sack and slips in two dried fish. No, they were not fried. They were dried, because they had to dry the perishable fish in order to preserve them.

So he took off to see the strange man. There are thousands and thousands of people, and because he's so little, he doubts he can make it to the front to be close to Jesus. He started weaving his way through the crowd, a little squeeze here, a little duck there, and he was in the front. That's what little kids do; I would do the same thing. No one wants to miss what is happening. He wants it all, so he made sure he was very close to where Christ was sitting. Why? Do you think he was the only little kid who had a really precious mommy who made him lunch? Don't just read the story; think about it. Do you think he was the only little boy in the crowd with a lunch? No. There were lots of little boys there with precious mothers who gave them all lunches. Question number two: Why did he behave quite the opposite of a little boy's nature? Little boys are so wonderful that they love to share their lunches, right? No, they steal other kids' lunches.

Think about it. You must *think*!

When I was in Belgium speaking one day, I made a little kid stand up. I said to the 11-year-old, "Would you share the lunch your mom gave you; would you share it with all of us here?" He was quiet for a moment, and then he said, "Yeah, I'd share." I knew he was sort of intimidated by his parents so he wanted to sound like a good little boy.

When I was in England, I asked another little boy, "Would you share your lunch?" He said, "No! It's *my* lunch."

So, why was this little boy in the story all of a sudden giving his lunch away, knowing full well he was not going to get a crumb? Why? Because he was sitting very close to Christ, and when Christ looked at the multitude, He was moved with compassion to feed them. He was concerned about their practical needs. That compassion rubbed off on the little boy and the little boy naturally wanted to help.

God is not all up in the air going to the seventh heaven all the time. God is not like that. God is Christ. God is absolutely practical. He knows when kids and elders are hungry and He wants to feed them. His head is not in clouds, and neither should ours be. So here was this little boy watching Christ, sitting very close so he could hear, and I believe he heard Christ ask Philip about buying food for these people. And he heard Philip's reply, "Ummm, you know, even if we had 200 denarii worth of bread [600 dollars; one year's wage for a man during that time], even that would not be enough to give them each a little piece of bread."

The little boy heard that and what did he do? He went up to Andrew, tugged on his shirt a little and said, "Hey, I got lunch. My mom made it for me. Do you think...do you think Christ would want to use it to feed the people?" He didn't go directly to Christ; he probably was nervous because he heard the guy was kind of strange.

Andrew could have told him, *"What? OK, strange little kid. You have a lunch. Good for you. Go sit down and eat your lunch. The rest of us don't have any, so you should be thankful you have lunch."* But good thing Andrew didn't think that. Rather, Andrew took the food and gave it to Christ and said, "Here, this lad gave his lunch, but it isn't much for all these people." Because of that last phrase, we know Andrew's doubt was evident.

But the little boy didn't doubt. No he didn't. He gave his lunch and then he sat down and watched Christ. *I wonder what*

He's going to do. I mean, at least my lunch could feed Christ. He was watching Christ the whole time. He saw Christ take the food, bless it, and give it out to the disciples, who turned to distribute it to the people. Do you think a little boy of 11 would just sit there quietly and think, Oh, that was very nice. No way! He would be shouting, "Hey, do you know that you're eating my lunch?! It was only five loaves and two fish! My mommy made it! My mom made it just this morning for me. And now Christ gave it to you. He broke it up, and He ʼblessed it…and now it's enough to feed all you people!"

He ran around from person to person, telling them excitingly, "Do you know my mom made this lunch? Can you believe that? You're actually eating my little lunch. Oh my goodness!" He was running around, and probably lost count of how many people were eating his lunch. Finally he was exhausted, and he said, "That's my lunch! Just five loaves of bread and two fish," He didn't know when his lunch was finished and when Christ's lunch began. He looked at Christ and marveled, *How could He do so much with so little? Who is this God? How could He do that?*

You know the leftover food that Jesus had the disciples pick up in 12 baskets? Do you think Christ would send the little boy home without a basket? In fact, where in the world did the baskets come from in the middle of nowhere? Ah ha! Think. Where did the baskets come from? People were carrying them. So were they carrying empty baskets around? No, they carried food in the baskets. Those baskets had food in them and I bet the people who owned those baskets ate the food. Think about it. Christ, this God of the Bible, He's a little bit different, isn't He? He is strange. He said, "It's all right. You ate your food? That's OK. Bring your empty basket and I will fill it up. And I'm sure He said, "Make sure the little boy gets a basket to take home to his mommy."

And what do you think his mom said when she saw the basket of food? "Wait a minute now, little John. I know what you did. You stole from the bakery, didn't you? Uh-huh. I know you're naughty. Don't you lie to me boy."

And the little boy desperately told his mommy, "I didn't steal it, Mom. You just have to hear what happened with the lunch you made me!"

"Oh, now you're going to make stories up, eh? Another story? Nope, I'm not impressed. I'm not listening."

And the little boy started to cry. "Mom...Mom, you don't know what happened today. I heard Christ say He needed food to feed the thousands of people who were there. And I don't know what happened to me, but I felt this wave of love hit me. I felt a need inside to do something. And so I...I...I just had to give my lunch to Christ—otherwise I think I would have gone crazy. I gave my lunch to one of His disciples, and I really didn't know if they would return it to me or scold me. But Christ took it, the great lunch you made me, Mom, and He actually blessed it. Then He gave it to all the people and those thousands of people ate, and they had leftovers, Mom. That man is really strange. He did that. That...that man. He did that!"

And his mother put her hand on her head and sat down on the mud floor and cried, "How could He? How could He do so much with so little? How?"

I could tell you hundreds and thousands of stories of people coming to know this Great Love of God! We don't need to do anything special except be a carrier of His love. It's effortless. Let's carry His love effortlessly worldwide, shall we? And the whole earth will be filled with His glorious love!

•　•　•

Please bow your heart.

We come before You; here we are. We have one pursuit, the pursuit of Your love; we have one goal, your great love. We don't want to make it any other thing, we Don't want to get distracted or deviated from running after Your love. Lord, You're looking for simple people. You're looking for little people with the simplicity of Your love, so that we can carry it to the uttermost part of the world, so we can carry it wherever we are.

No matter how dark it is, Lord, we will not just sit in the darkness and complain about how dark it is. I pray, God, that we would get up and light the candle of Your great love. May we be the ones to stand up and love. May we be found faithful as the hearts of men and women grow cold. May we be found with hearts warmed with Your love. We dedicate ourselves afresh and we cry out for Your love in Christ's precious name.

Endnotes

1. Youngbee Dale, "India: Thousands of Children as Young as Four Are Sold to Hindu Temples for Sexual Exploitation," Examiner.com, http://www.examiner.com/human-rights-in-national/india-thousands-of-children-as-young-as-four-are-sold-to-hindu-temples-for-sexual-exploitation, (accessed August 20, 2011).

2. Aleksandr Solzhenitsyn, Goodreads website, "Aleksandr I. Solzhenitsyn > Quotes > Quotation Source: The Gulag Archipelago: 1918-1956," http://www.goodreads.com/author/quotes/10420.Aleksandr_Solzhenitsyn, (accessed August 20, 2011).

Chapter 7

WITCHES, BABIES, AND SOLDIERS

by Will Hart

EVERYWHERE YOU GO YOU BRING the Kingdom with you. You are revival. Until the Church realizes that, we are going to miss opportunities. Why? Because the same Spirit who raised Christ from the dead lives in us, breathes in us, works through us, and flows through us! It's you with Him! Is it about you? No. But there is a unity in God coming and working with us.

He says, "Listen, you are broken vessels." I say, "Great, He uses broken vessels. He uses imperfect people. He uses people with no education, with no training." I failed Spanish three times in high school. Three times! But when the King came into me, I picked up Spanish in six months.

I visited Paraguay for two weeks on a brief ministry trip, and during those two weeks I saw God move. I saw the power of God flow through me. It was amazing. While I was there, the Lord said, "This is the place I want you to be." After I returned home, I told my parents, "Mom, Dad, I feel like I'm supposed to move to Paraguay."

"But you don't speak the language. Do you know the people you are going to stay with?" they asked.

"No, I have no idea who they are, but I met them for a second at an event, and I think it'll be OK," I said confidently.

Off I went, and I moved into the closet in a house of a pastor I had never met. So often we wait for a beautiful picture, a gift to fall in our laps before we respond, but the reality is sometimes you have to fight for things. Sometimes you have to take risks. I didn't know what I was doing. Part of it may have been just plain stupidity—but God can use that too, if your heart is right.

We are in the middle of a journey with the King. You are in the middle of it. It's not always a beautiful picture. It's not always picture-perfect. It doesn't always make sense. Since when does our faith rely on what makes sense? Come on! Seriously? When does it all have to make sense? I love it when it does, but if my faith rests on that alone, I'll never go anywhere, I'll never do anything, I'll never accomplish these things for the Lord. I'm telling you, it doesn't always have to make sense. It didn't make sense when I moved into a closet in this pastor's house. I actually lived in a closet. It was weird. They threw a mattress in there and that was it.

I was 17 years old. I didn't speak the language. I had some bagpipes and some clothes and that's it. I didn't know what I was thinking. But I was hungry. I was hungry to be used. I was hungry to go after what God had for me. I was listening to that still, small voice, and that thing in my spirit that said, "Go." It didn't come as a booming from Heaven. "YOU ARE GOING TO PARAGUAY, WILL, AND THERE YOU WILL SEE MIGHTY SIGNS AND WONDERS!"

No, it didn't come that way.

I used to lay in bed at night weeping. I would cry, "God, what the heck am I doing here? Why am I here? What is this place?" And then miracles started to happen. We started receiving phone calls from the hospital. I don't know how it happened but they heard about us—the pastor and me. One time a man called my cell phone. He was speaking Spanish so I tossed it over to the pastor I was staying with. He said, "OK, OK, OK." We actually communicated by me typing in an English word or phrase and then hitting "Translate," and he would read what came up on the screen. That's how we would get along until I learned the language.

"There's a man whose son is in a coma. He wants us to come pray for him; he's about to die," the pastor told me.

We hopped into his little car and we drove to the hospital. They wouldn't allow us into the emergency room. But we didn't care what they said, and the father kind of snuck us into intensive care where his boy was. He was about 15 or 16 years of age and lying on the bed hooked up to every sort of machine that the hospital had. His head was swollen to twice the normal size, full of fluids. We learned that when they went in to cut out a tumor, they made scrambled eggs of his brain, and he slipped into a coma. Gone. He was in a coma for three months. The father was weeping, "What do I do? He's my son. I'm losing my son!"

That's a heavy load. At 17, I had never prayed for anyone so desperate before. I didn't know what I was doing. I was saved only six months prior. What to do? How should I pray? No ten-step manual would help me out at that point. I had to get real with God. "God, come. Come! Come into this place. Come into this room right now. Touch Your child." I had gone into hospitals before and prayed for people and they died. One guy died as I was praying for him. It was the worst! What a way to start off a healing ministry.

We were around the son's bed praying for just a few minutes when some hospital staff came running in. "Who are you? Why are you here?" You know, blah, blah, blah. And they kicked us out. We got back into the car and drove home. About two hours later, we received a phone call from the father and he was weeping. When I heard him weep, I thought to myself, *Oh no, I killed another one.*

"My son, my son! He's up!" the father said through tears of joy. About two hours after we left, the son sat straight up in bed and two liters of liquid drained from his brain. They moved him from intensive care into physical therapy. Bang—all that in one day. You don't have to know what you're doing. Get over it. Get over yourself. Since when was the Gospel about us? You don't have to know; you just have to step out in faith.

Keep It Simple

Come on. Keep it simple. You just have to be available. We saw so many amazing things. Word got around that God was healing people. We traveled all over Paraguay, and we saw some of the most amazing miracles. Kids would be taken up into Heaven; people were having out-of-body experiences; miracles, signs, and wonders started manifesting. You name it and it happened! A cloud of the anointing would show up in the meetings. I've seen the physical cloud of the anointing three times in my life, and twice it was in Paraguay. It was just amazing stuff.

Witches would come out to our meetings. We had this one girl, Delilah, who was an 18-year-old, blood-drinking witch. She met us outside of the church after an amazing, powerful service. God was moving so powerfully. As we were exiting the church,

Delilah was standing there and you could just see the demonic influence in her eyes. I had never seen deliverance. I had never met a witch before. And there she was on the sidewalk saying, "You guys are David Copperfield. You guys are just magicians. I know what real power is."

"Oh, yeah?" we said. We went right up to her to lay hands on her. Back then, I was usually the one who "caught" the person. Most people fall down under the power of God, so when my friend Bob would lay hands on someone, I was the catcher. So Bob went to lay hands on Delilah, and I was sure God would touch her. I had never been around the demonic in that form before, and as she started going backward, I said, "Yeah, Holy Ghost! Get her, God, get her!" And Delilah was going back and all of a sudden her claws came up and she was snarling and hissing and clawing. I was like, "Whoa! What happened?"

Bob said, "Get in the car, Will. It's time. We've got to go. We don't have time to do this."

"What?" I said. "This is what we're supposed do. Help the oppressed!"

"Listen, this one will take a little bit more than just a quick prayer."

And we left. That was the demonic. It was the first time I had ever seen it. It totally freaked me out. It's normal to be scared.

We went back to the church the next day for a series of meetings and when we looked at the front of the church, there was Delilah. She was standing there with her arms lifted to the King, worshiping. Delilah and her brother were there worshiping—full-blown, gone in worship to Jesus.

No one could figure out what was going on, so we went to talk to her. "What are you doing here? What's going on?" we asked her. She turned with tears in her eyes and we saw that something had happened.

Delilah explained, "I was very angry when you saw me outside the church. As soon as I calmed down, I grabbed my brother and we were walking home. As we rounded the corner, we looked up and in the window of the church there was a man standing there dressed in white. I've never experienced fear like that in my entire life. We grabbed each other's hands and took off running. We were petrified."

As they were running, they heard footsteps behind them. They ran into their house, and they closed the doors, closed the windows, and they were clutching each other on the floor in the center of the room. Then a wind came in and a picture of Jesus was put up on the wall. And they said, "The Holy Spirit led us through the prayer of salvation right then and there." They dedicated their lives to the Lord on the floor, holding each other. Amazing!

What God is doing is greater than what we can do. As you come into alignment with Him, He does amazing things. Delilah got radically saved, radically transformed. She actually became a member of our ministry team. And I actually fell in love with my wife because of Delilah. We got most of her critters out, but there were a couple that were a little harder to get. We were all at a service and Delilah was helping out with ministry when she started to manifest. This thing came up inside of her and she lunged out and grabbed this other young woman, who was our translator at the time. Delilah grabbed her face with her claws. I didn't know what's going on, and I watched this young woman as she took Delilah's hand and pushed it to the side and said, "Peace in Jesus' name." Delilah crumbled on the floor sobbing and weeping, delivered instantly right then and there. I thought, *That's the woman I want!*

Trust in God

It's OK not to understand what's going on. Why? Because then we trust in God. We trust in who He says He is, and we trust in the fact that He will back us up when we step out. You just have to have the heart to go. You have to align yourself with what He's calling you to do.

Why am I sharing all this stuff with you? So you can read cool stories? No! We have had enough cool stories. I want this to increase your faith. I want you to go and do something with what you are receiving. If you don't, we fail. My goal is to work myself out of a job. It's my mission statement. It's my vision. I don't want to have to do what I do. Why? I want the Church to get it. It's easy! Come on! Why are you here? It's time that we rise up, that we stop making excuses.

At one point in our lives, we felt like God had called us to Africa, not partially, not 50 percent, but full-on called us there; and we wanted to fulfill that calling. And we really felt strongly. My wife and I talked about how to follow His leading. How were we going to do this with children? "Lord, if you are calling us here, then I believe we are to have our children here." It was as simple as that. It was this simple word going on faith, "God, I feel like we are supposed to have our children here." It didn't make any sense in the world, right?

I turned to my wife and said, "Listen, whatever it costs, whatever it takes, I will take you back to wherever you want to go. We can go to Paraguay, to the States, to South Africa, wherever; let's just not have the baby delivered here." She said, "No, I feel like this is the place we are supposed to have our son." The months go on and my wife got more and more beautiful. We thought we needed a game plan, so we prayed, "God, how are we going to do this delivery?" As soon as we did, there was a knock at our door. It was a doctor, a missionary from Iris Ministries in Mozambique. It was amazing. She had been the doctor for 250 births.

Thank You, Lord! You have provided this amazing doctor; the perfect fit for our scenario. Our house is made out of bamboo and rocks with cement and a tin roof and it is located in rural, northern Mozambique—it is very remote. So we start getting our supplies together for the birth. We were just a few weeks away from the birth and past the point when she could fly. There was no more getting on planes. No more transportation. The deal was done.

Two weeks before the due date, there was a knock on the door. It was the doctor. She said, "Will, I have great news and I have really bad news. I just received a job offer to become the head of medicine over a major Christian college back in the States. The bad news is I have to leave tomorrow."

And in a moment, our well-thought-out plans disappeared. What to do? We had to stand on the Word. We were missionaries. We didn't have any money. What to do? I looked at my truck. *Maybe I can put a bed in the back of my truck and we can make the six-day journey driving over some of the worst roads on the planet and maybe get her to South Africa where there are hospitals. But what if she goes into labor on the ride? If anything would induce labor it would be that journey.*

What to do? We prayed. Soon afterward, a girl came up to us and said, "I'm 18 years old and my name is Leah. I've done many deliveries."

"Really? How many?" I asked.

"Well, I've done about four deliveries."

I said, "Come on, girl. You're on board. You're part of the team!" We also had a friend, Yanni, who is like a nurse practitioner. She had seen a couple of births, but never was part of the delivery. Along with the Bible, we had a birthing book too. It had good advice like putting a plastic bag down on the floor so the baby wouldn't fall on the dirt when it came out. I mean it was crazy. With only a couple of days to go, our team was ready.

Then all of a sudden, Leah said something happened at home and she took a flight back. Now it was just my wife, Yanni, and me. Yanni is a bright, amazing girl, but she hadn't done any births up to that point. What to do? I read the book cover to cover.

When I returned from swimming Saturday morning, my wife was standing in the doorway. "They're about ten minutes apart. Let's go to the beach." So we got in the truck and we motored 45 minutes down through the bush to this secret beach that we had. It was awesome. We ate chicken there. It was great. After a couple of hours, she was giving me the thumbs down sign from her beach chair as I was out swimming. As we were driving back to the missionary base, this fear came over us and we realized, "Uh-oh, there's no backing out now."

I dropped my wife off at the house and took Yanni to the ministry's medical clinic. We started tearing that place apart. I was grabbing aspirin, Tylenol PM, anything that looked like it could be good for babies. We motored back home, and it began. One hour, two hours, three hours, four hours, six hours, eight hours, ten hours. At about the ten-hour mark, we had no idea what was taking place. I was probably the most scared I have ever been in my entire life. The only way that my wife could get medically evacuated was by a plane coming from South

Africa—about a five-hour journey, one way. And they won't even take off from the runway unless they have $25,000 wired into their bank account, and that takes about two days to happen in Africa.

Fear hit us. I thought I was going to lose my wife. I kicked everyone out of the room, and I got down by her bed, and I wrapped my arms around her. "I am so sorry," I told her.

Have you ever felt like you missed God? I had never felt like that before. *What if I made the biggest mistake of our lives? Not only will I lose the one I love, but I'll also lose our firstborn.* A prayer of faith didn't come out. I just said, "I'm so sorry. I'm so sorry. God, please, please do something."

Then I remembered the phone number of a Cuban doctor I had met downtown. He was visiting the clinic. I called him at four in the morning. I said, "Please come. My wife is in labor. We don't know what's happening. Come quickly." When he arrived, my wife was ready to kill everything and everyone. "Help me! Cut the baby out of me!" The doctor laughed at my wife and peace came into the room. It was the craziest thing. We all took a big, deep breath. Then he spoke to her in her native language, "You're going to be just fine, girl." In her native language. Come on, out of all the languages in the world, she got a Spanish-speaking doctor in rural Mozambique?

Within a half hour, our son Joshua entered this world. It was one of the scariest moments of my life. But God came through— He always comes through.

Have No Fear

Listen, He's not dangling you out there in life. He's not leading you into something where He will not back you up. I'm telling you, you would think we had learned our lesson, but we didn't. We had our daughter Bella there, too. God is not going to lead you astray. He's not going to put you out there alone. And even if you do get put out there, and you miss it, Daddy comes and He picks up the pieces. Daddy comes and makes it all better.

Even in our stupidity, He comes. Why? Because you are His son; because you are His daughter. He comes and puts the pieces together. He will not leave you stranded. He will not leave out there alone. He will not leave you dangling. Daddy's job is to take care of His children. Whether you want Him to or not. My children do not have to ask me. *Hello?* I already know. They just come running up to me with their big eyes, and I say, "Whatever you want is yours. Just have it. You can have it." They don't even have to ask. I come running just as fast when they scream at the top of their lungs as when they are silent.

So many of us are used to screaming at the top of our lungs. Daddy comes the same when you are quiet. He comes because He is the Father and you are His kid. He comes. Fear cannot direct us. It can't tell us what to do or where to go and how to do it. It cannot. It does not play a role in the decisions that we make with the King of kings and Lord of lords. It's what holds us back. *Fear is faith in the enemy.* Fear is believing in the lie of the enemy over your life. Listen, what God says supersedes all of that. *Oh, but Will, it doesn't make sense.* Come on, it doesn't have to. It doesn't have to make sense. Just go.

I never experienced fear like I did on my trip to the Congo. It was one of the most amazing experiences and times of our lives. Heidi Baker of Iris Ministries was sending a team and I wanted to go. But I did not want to take my wife. Why? The Congo is one of the most dangerous territories on the planet. When we were there, the largest United Nations troop force in the world was located in the Congo. Rebels were fiercely fighting. It was absolutely a horrible place. So I went to my wife, "Babe, I'm going to the Congo for a month, a month and a half. We're going to buy some land and build an orphanage."

She says, "Guess what, I'm going to come with you. You're not hearing God."

I said, "I think I am. It's too dangerous for you to go. Listen, I'm going to go and pray, and I'm going to ask the Lord, and He's going to tell me. He'll direct me, and it will be good. So I will see you in about 15." I went into my little room and said, "OK, God, fix my wife please. I think she's broken right now. God, do you want my wife to go?"

The Lord spoke to me audibly at this point. I've only had a few times when I've heard His audible voice and this was one of them. He said, "Will, true life in Me comes from the understanding that this life doesn't belong to you. Freedom in me comes when you get it through your thick head [He didn't actually say "thick head"] that you're not the one running the show. What makes you think that she's safer with you here in rural, northern Mozambique than with you in the Congo?

I said, "But God, it makes sense."

He says, "It makes sense to *you*."

I started thinking to myself, *Being in northern Africa, in the middle of nowhere, she would be safer? It's not like anybody couldn't just walk up to the front door of our house in Mozambique and just stab her. My sister lives in Mozambique, and she's been stabbed. She has a huge stab scar on her arm; she was just walking down the street. What makes me think that she's safer at home?*

Come on, don't we do that though? We try to justify our choices in our minds. I told my wife I was sorry and we went to the Congo together. It was amazing. We saw the Book of Acts take place in Congo. If you saw the movie *Hotel Rwanda,* you saw the Hutus and the Tutsis warring. The Hutu rebels, after they battled in Rwanda, fled into the Congo and developed more groups. There was, when we were there, about 25 different rebel groups functioning in the Congo. It was incredibly dangerous, and here we were, four whiteys just cruising around, just preaching the Gospel. We preached on boats. We preached on the lava flows. The churches were made out of lava rocks.

When God says He's going to open it up, He follows through. I went from ministering on the streets and in these churches, to going on the radio on the largest Christian radio network in the entire country. I preached to the entire country at one time. When God says He's going to put you in front of thousands and thousands, He does it, in a moment.

And we preached the Gospel and told these people that we were going to go visit a certain village, about 60 miles from where we were staying. We were going to be there in about four or five days. We were going to hold a conference and buy land to build an orphanage. We took off in our car four or five days later. It was about 60 miles away, so we thought we would arrive in a couple of hours. It took us about six hours to get to the entranceway of the park. As we pulled up to the national park, soldiers surrounded our car. I had my wife there with me, and I was frightened for her. The soldiers are half the problem in that country. They were handed weapons at a young age and told to fight when the time comes. The soldiers aren't fed or clothed— the government doesn't take care of them—but they are commanded to devote their lives to the army. I was told by a UN worker that 50 percent of rapes are by Congolese soldiers.

It is such a blessing to live in a country where you can call 911 and the police are there within ten or fifteen minutes. The

Congo is dark. Like total, total darkness, and nothing can be relied upon. There is no such thing as relying on other people to come and help you when the time comes. It is every person for themselves. The mentality is crazy; it's like nothing in the Western world.

So these soldiers were surrounding our cars and they told us that we were about to drive through rebel territory. The rebels had been flowing through this jungle. They said they heard on the radio that we were coming and wanted to give us protection. The next thing we knew, we had soldiers in our cars with rocket launchers as we drove into this jungle. And then the cars started to break down. The roads were the worst you could possibly imagine. The journey that was only supposed to take a few hours went into four, six, eight, ten hours and it was getting darker and darker. And there was no turning back because the roads were not wide enough. We were driving along cliffs on a muddy road at angles where we could easily slip off and crash below.

The two vehicles were covered in mud and every few miles we got stuck. We would spend 20 minutes to an hour digging ourselves out, only to move on to the next mud hole where we would get stuck again. Then we come around a corner, and in the middle of the road, blocking everything, was a massive truck piled 20 feet high with charcoal. We couldn't turn around or go forward. All of us tried and tried to push the truck, but nothing worked.

All the while I was looking for an escape route so I could hide my wife so she wouldn't get raped if the soldiers came. That's what you go through; the emotions are intense. All these things were going through my mind and then I heard a noise in the distance. Not the sound I wanted to hear. A group came around the bend wearing purple and white robes that were completely covering their bodies. The first thing I noticed was a purple cross on their chests. It was a group of villagers who heard we were coming and got scared when we didn't show up.

They had taken the last of their money, pooled it together, and sewed choir robes out of scrap material. When they saw us, they came running, picked us up on their shoulders, and then set us down rejoicing. There we were in the middle of rebel territory being spun around by these Christian Congolese. There was no electricity, no running water, nothing. These were the poorest of the poor and they lived in one of the most dangerous places in the world. There on the front lines, they were spinning around rejoicing with us.

Like an army, these men pushed the charcoal truck out of the mud and it went barreling down the road. Finally we entered the village and it was pitch black. They didn't care. Everyone was there. Everyone had gathered. People had walked for four days, through rebel territory, with no shoes, nothing. They came because they heard on the radio that the Gospel was going to be preached. They came at much risk to their lives and they surrounded us. We preached by candlelight. There was no running water, no electricity, no microphones, just the Gospel and our voices. I'll never forget it. It was the most glorious service I've ever been a part of.

The Holy Spirit fell in that pitch-blackness. The next morning we got up and there were so many people. They were surrounding us. There was a tent made out of bamboo and UN tarps. Then God showed up. We felt the Holy Spirit moving, and as I was sitting in the front getting ready to speak, I looked out at this beautiful group of people. There was a man sitting in the front row on a log and he looked different to me. He just looked different. And as I was sitting there, I got a word for him—bang! It just came flooding in. I got this word from God, and it wasn't a small word. It wasn't like, "Hey, Jesus loves you, man. Read your Bible."

No. It was a great word; it was huge; it was about how he was called to be a pastor and how God had given him this congregation, but it didn't look like a normal congregation. I saw him standing with the government. I even saw him standing alongside the president. "How can this be God? We're out in the middle of nowhere; how can I give him this word?"

As I turned to my wife, she looked at me and said, "You need to prophesy over that man."

As I was prophesying over him, the Holy Spirit hit him. He loved it! The power of God fell and was flowing through him as we prophesied destiny over him. Then I heard the Lord telling me to call in all the Congolese soldiers. So I stood up and I told every soldier to come. I didn't know this when we were there, but this place bordered rebel territory and the Congolese soldiers had an outpost there. They were fighting the Hutu rebels right there, and we were on the front lines. The whole town was full of soldiers. I said, "Every soldier within the sound of my voice, get in here now! God is going to touch you!" One by one, they dropped their guns and they started lining up in the church.

Does this spark your heart for missions? If anything, will these stories spark a passion in you to get out of your comfort zone?

The poorest of the poorest of the poorest of the poor heard a word over the radio, a 20-minute message over the radio, and dropped everything. They were hungry for the Gospel. They were hungry for more. And the soldiers, one by one, start getting blasted by the Holy Spirit. The Holy Spirit was flowing through these guys. My greatest fear was for danger to come against my family. My greatest fear was for danger to come against my wife. I don't care about my life, but as long as I live I'll do whatever it takes to keep that woman safe. My greatest fear was for her life. Remember the man that I prophesied over in the beginning of that service? He came running up to me and said, "You don't know who I am. I'm the captain of the Congolese Army over this entire area, and I just got saved two weeks ago."

Wow!

• • •

Holy Spirit, I thank You for Your people. Jesus, I thank You for what You're doing. God, I thank You for the move of Your spirit over our lives and in our hearts. And Lord, I ask that You would come. Lord, that You would come and use us. God, I ask that You would raise up missionaries. God, I ask that You would raise up men and women who will lay down their lives for nothing but You, nothing but Your Kingdom. God, I ask that You would raise up ones who will give their lives for Africa, for Asia, for the Middle East, for Europe, and for America. God, I pray that they will lay down their lives for their state, for their city, for their jobs, and for their workplace. God, I ask that You break all fear now in Jesus' name. Come, Holy Spirit. Come, Holy Spirit. Thank You, Father. In Jesus' name, amen.

Chapter 8

STEPPING INTO YOUR DESTINY

by Angela Greenig

GOD SAYS HE IS GOING to knock down every wall that the enemy has built up. I believe that God wants to start knocking down the walls in your families and in your neighborhoods— He's going to knock down the sickness, the disease, and all the lies of the enemy. Instead of being a prisoner in bondage, you can use that knocked-down wall as a stepping-stone into your freedom. All of our walls and all of our wars are different because we all come from different backgrounds with different experiences and different obstacles. You must choose and create and set the boundaries for your life that will allow the walls to come down and to stay down. The Father said it wouldn't be easy. He also says if you step out and walk on water and keep focused on Him, you will not fail.

I was born in 1958 and I was raped the first time in 1962 when I was four. By the time I was 9 years old I was dealing drugs. My life was in a continuous downhill spiral. I cannot tell you how many times I tried to commit suicide. I started self-medicating, using anything to escape my reality. I was a junkie—doing drugs, drinking alcohol. I became a stripper and then a prostitute. My entire life was nothing but war and darkness; my family is Mafia on one side and Indian on the other. I was 21 when I first heard about the everlasting life and unconditional love of Jesus Christ. When I got saved, it was radical because of the darkness I dwelt in. God said to me, "Daughter, you have been pinned against this wall. It's time for the wall to come down—and for you to step out." And I've been stepping out for about 28 years now. If God could take the hand of the person that I was and pull me out of darkness, He can and will do it for you if you allow Him to.

We must learn how to step out. You may be disgusted and frustrated and struggling to get by. Micah 7:1 says, *"Woe is me!"* (NKJV). But I don't think so. This doesn't have to be your plight today or any day because God has given each of His children extreme gifts and mandates and mantles. God wants to activate you. You have to start stirring up your faith—even if that means talking to yourself in the mirror and encouraging yourself every day by saying, "I'm a warrior for Jesus Christ. I have purpose and destiny." Even if no one else believes it, I know that God believes in me—and that's all that matters because I am telling you that God believes in you.

There to Kill Me

I have gone through horrific circumstances, and I have had legions of demons—trust me. No one laid hands on me for my deliverance. You can experience deliverance from your bondage; you can experience the love of the Father and the spirit of adoption. You can have a mind at peace. You do not need to spend money for conferences thinking that so-and-so needs to pray for you or lay hands on you for you to be set free. We all have the fullness of the Father available to us, and He will meet us right where we are at. I pressed through until I got my answer and Jesus set me free. You too can be set free from whatever it is that binds you if you press through to Jesus. I know you might be saying, "But Angela, I've prayed and I've prayed and God is not healing me." KEEP PRESSING! I promise you, if your thirst cannot be quenched by anything but Jesus, then Jesus you will find. Search for Him with a desire that is greater than anything you have ever known and you WILL find Him; He is waiting for you!

This is your key: fear keeps people bound. Fear is False Evidence Appearing Real. The enemy bombards the minds of people and reminds them of their past and that keeps them in bondage. We need to kick down the walls that bind us in our prison. How do you kick down those walls? You take that lie the enemy is telling you and replace it with truth from God's Word. You find that verse that speaks truth and you memorize it and you speak it out over and over and over until you believe it.

One day I was heading into Baltimore, Maryland, with the Catholic Church to teach on warfare, deliverance, and healing. There was an individual that bled the stigmata there (blood flowing from locations corresponding to the crucifixion wounds of Jesus) so this teaching was desperately needed. I had worked with the Church for several years teaching on the demonic and the bondage that comes with not knowing who you are in Christ. I was on my way to the airport when I received a call that there was an emergency. This is how I met Esther. I was told that Esther was in need of help and she was on her way to the house. Esther was covered in hordes of darkness. As I was driving to the house, I was about ten minutes away and I started to physically feel ill. I knew that she was in trouble and I started praying and warring. When I got to the house, I explained the darkness that I felt was coming. I could see in the spirit that she was being pulled by seven black horses and when she arrived at the house, she blew open the door without touching it. Her eyes were completely black; there was no white to be found...literally.

She had a choice to make. She could be sucked into the depths of hell, which is exactly where satan wanted her, or she could choose Jesus Christ and a new life. When she heard about this choice she needed to make, it was like a little girl who broke free for a split second and she said, "Help me." Esther was sent there to kill me to keep me from going and teaching in Baltimore. She was told that there had to be an opening for them to get in, and so far none could be found. So Esther asked permission to find the opening. That is why the attempt was made. The day she stepped out to kill me was the day that she allowed Jesus to take her by the hand and pull her out of her darkness.

Esther is a former satanist. She eventually came to know the Lord in a big way. This is her story:

It was a process for me to come to the Lord; it wasn't a sudden and easy transformation. For me, it was and is a continual renewal of my mind. It's like a totally new hard drive being put in your brain. I had to surround myself with people who spoke life into me and were going to love me regardless if I fell on my face. I had not just one but a few deliverances.

In the beginning it was like hell for me. Every night for a year and a half I was so tormented in my mind that I couldn't sleep. Sometimes I would think, *Oh my God. Woe is me.* And I'd start ripping at my wounds; I was a very wounded person. Then I realized that I couldn't build my house in hell and survive. I had to walk through it—step away from it—and I received supernatural strength from Papa, from Abba Father up above, and from the people slapping me on the back of my head, saying, "Pull yourself together. Stop licking your wounds."

Rather than listening to the demonic crap that speaks lies to your head, I choose to listen to the angels. I had to learn to trust God and not be moved by circumstances but only by the throne of God. I put sticky notes everywhere, arming myself with Scripture. "I am beautiful. I will make it." Words of life. Proclamations. I was going to start walking in the purpose that God had for me. And I was going to start loving other people and myself. Because that's what it's about. It's about loving.

There are a lot of satanists out there just like me who want to get out, but they don't know how. It's like the Mafia; you don't get out alive without consequences. The Church must be willing to open up our hearts and lift up our homes and sacrifice everything to bring God's children out of the depths of hell. And as I speak this truth, it comes with a high price. To accept Jesus costs you everything. If you are willing to lay down your life as a sacrifice to Him, He will totally bless you and give you the strength to persevere—to move into His blessings and walk toward your destiny. Yes, you still have your trials and difficult circumstances, but the primary thing is to keep your focus on the goal. The main prize is walking in the destiny that God prepared for you. We don't go into the battle naked. We must put on the armor. We have to renew our minds. We have to speak life out.

Fear and Deception

There are 16 demonic spirits because there are 16 Major and Minor Prophets in the Old Testament. Again, satan counters everything of God. His goal is to kill, steal, and destroy (see John 10:10). Let me share a couple of these with you. He uses a lying spirit, which is the godfather of the underworld. Without the lie you have nothing. This spirit's job is to pervert the truth. Every day I bind the lying spirit by commanding him to shut his mouth. The perverse spirit is not always about sexual matters. Manifestations of the perverse spirit include wounded spirits, entrapments, self-lovers, false teachers, and moodiness. Romans 1:17-32 speaks of this spirit. It is to be bound, cast out, and replaced with the Holy Spirit. It is important to stay armed up (see Eph. 6:13-17).

Every day put on your armor because any offense opens the door to deception. Once the door is open, the spirit of detraction enters. It can cause strife, destruction, discord, division, and defamation. These are a few of the manifestations of this spirit. This spirit is like a clock that goes backward to sow and bring in division. It will not allow lives to continue in peace, but likes to disturb them. Every day I bind these three spirits: the lying so that truth will prevail, the perverse so there will be no twisting of words or actions or offenses coming in, and I bind the spirit of detraction so these three things will not work together to destroy myself, my family, my friends, or ministry.

Isaiah 61:3 talks about the spirit of heaviness. Those with this spirit will be depressed, lonely, discouraged, feel rejected, and abandoned. Because of my sexual abuse as a child, I ate hoping to be left alone, hoping that the abuse would stop—but it didn't. My circumstances in the natural were because of the spiritual war. The more weight I gained, the more depressed I got. The heaviness was wickedly compounded. It shifted and I became anorexic and bulimic. The spirit of heaviness is the only spirit that a person is able to control in their physical appearance. People may look at someone who is affected by the spirit of heaviness and assume that it is bondage or fear, and yes it is bondage, but it is rooted in the spirit of heaviness. It is so easy for us to look at someone in the natural and not even realize the spirits they are dealing with in the spiritual realm. For example, when I was overweight from overeating, people would look at me and wonder why I just couldn't lose weight.

We need focus. We need to pray that God will give us spiritual eyes to see each other as God sees us. Where is the compassion? If you hate the devil, you better have passion and compassion for God's people. We need to step out and do the work of the Lord. I always tell people to read the Bible when they want to learn. Understand what you're dealing with. We can't go off half-cocked and start shooting things, claiming there's a demon behind every rock! He said, "I've given you all power and authority and dominion to subdue the enemy." We need discernment and wisdom, not to keep our focus on the enemy but to see the goodness that is God. As we renew our minds and become more like Christ, we will learn to walk in holiness and righteousness.

Power From God

Micah 3:8 is one of my key Scripture verses. It says, *"But as for me, I am filled with power, with the Spirit of the Lord, and with justice and might, to decree to Jacob his transgression, and to Israel his sin."* God kept telling me, "But I have filled you with power." God says, "Listen, you are filled with My power. It's not by might or by power, but it's by My Spirit says the Lord" (see Zech. 4:6). And when you start to hear and move and breathe and be in Him, and stay humble before Him, and do the will and the work that He's called you to do, you will be setting yourself and others free in no time.

Another empowering Scripture passage is Jude 1:24-25:

To him who is able to keep you from stumbling and to present you before his glorious presence without fault and with great joy—to the only God our Savior be glory, majesty, power and authority, through Jesus Christ our Lord, before all ages, now and forevermore! Amen.

The bottom line is that we are to take back what belongs to us. We are to conquer and bring back into submission what God gave us through His Son Jesus Christ, though the cross, through the blood, through the pain that He went through for reconciliation. He doesn't want us walking around in death clothes; He has reconciled us to new life.

Isaiah 9 talks about the Prince of Peace. He is Mighty God, Beauty, and King. But in that Word, it also decrees to take off the bloody garments of your past. Take them off. Don't keep wearing things that you think have made you who you are today. Because of Jesus, you are power and authority. You are war, and you are peace. If you want peace, it's going to come with war. There was peace in Heaven and then war hit the earth. We are still in a battle for truth and justice.

To the things that happened when you were young and mistreated, maybe beaten, raped, tortured, or whatever you have gone through, He says, *"That's who you were."* In Second Corinthians 5:17, Paul tells us that, *"if anyone is in Christ, he is a new creation; old things have passed away; behold, all things have become new"* (NKJV). This is who you are now. The problem is you don't believe it. You don't really love yourself, because if you truly loved yourself, you would look in the mirror and see what

Christ sees. Christ sees someone who is fearfully and wonderfully made, someone who was born with his or her destiny already laid in the foundation of Christ. He has given you great hope and future, and He has plans to prosper you and not harm you. He sees someone who was created in His image, whose mind is renewing into the mind of Christ.

The greatest weapon is from within. It's inside you; you have the Holy Spirit. The devil is very good at his job. He has been around a lot longer than you and me. My husband and I divorced once because the enemy just knocked us out—and we didn't even see it coming. Oh brother, sister, holier than thou, let that be a word to you. Be aware of the devil's tactics because he is sneaky and subtle. Unless you put your armor on and diligently stand watch over yourself and your family, friends, and ministry, and fervently pray and intercede, anyone is susceptible. See, we weren't standing guard, and we were doing things the way we thought we should be doing them, and not the way God wanted us to do it.

Once we got it, once we understood what areas needed to be set free, and we pressed into Him and His will, everything shifted. And I've done it His way ever since. God is not going to dump everything in your lap at one time. There is no list of things that He will ask you to change in order to be used by Him. He will work one thing at a time. I still wasn't healed from my past, and in order for my marriage to truly become intertwined with God, I still had things to work on. Because of being raped and abused, our marriage was a joke. Many Christians are really messed up when it comes to marriage and sex. Let's just be real. They're having problems communicating. They're frustrated. They get jealous and envious because the husband or the wife is stepping out. Many are in a constant battle, which the devil loves. But if we get into the Word, we will understand who

God is. God is love, and when we fully grasp the love of Christ, we can do anything.

Your Choice

You must understand who you are in Christ. You have to make a choice. Your spouse can't choose, your kids can't choose, your pastor or your neighbor can't choose for you. When you choose to follow Christ, and you choose to seek a relationship with Him, He and only He will show you what your ministry is. Not somebody else who says, "Well, I think you're called into evangelism, or pastoring, or whatever." Something will spark in you if you're called to that ministry—trust me. You won't be able to stop yourself. For example, I want every demonic hot spot conquered, and I have a dream to accomplish just that. I want to raise up a remnant of 300 worldwide. I said, "Lord, I'm going to train up people to take down satanic camps." My desire is to see those who satan has planned for hell come to life in Christ.

You are in the army of God and God is calling you in. There are five uses for a shofar, and one of them is for warfare. Are you willing to be a warrior for Him? In the name of the Father and of the Son and of the Holy Spirit, Father, this day we dig a pit for the enemy. This battle cry is taken from Psalm 94. God says the enemy cannot come out of the pit that we dig. And Lord, we decree that Your Kingdom come, Your will be done on earth as it is in Heaven. We come against every curse, every incantation that would raise itself up against the name of Jesus Christ. God, we ask today that You will forgive us because we have watered down Your Word. And as warriors of the Most High God, we have been known to run and hide.

Too many of God's people have fallen asleep and they are not ready for the battle that is already raging. Because we are so busy, we have no time to pray or be with the Father, and we have no time to study and to strategize. We have got to start stepping out and you must choose to do so. You have to make time for Christ! You know why we are bound? Because we are not stepping out, we are not trusting God, and we don't know who we are in Christ. We are not renewing our mind. The lying spirit seduces and tells us that we are worth nothing. I believed that lie all my life until I accepted Jesus as Savior. In fact, I had a teacher that told me I would grow up to be nothing. And that's what I was. She said I was stupid and I believed it. Life and death is in the power of your tongue (see Prov. 18:21). As a person speaks, so you will become—unless you listen only to God. Only He knows your full potential.

So do not throw away your confidence; it will be richly rewarded. You need to persevere so that when you have done the will of God, you will receive what he has promised. For, "In just a little while, He who is coming will come and will not delay" (Hebrews 10:35-37).

Listen, we are throwing away our confidence. Don't lose hope and don't lose faith. Just because somebody doesn't get healed right away, don't throw your confidence or your faith away. I prayed for 99 people who didn't get healed out of their wheelchairs. I was ready to give up. I was so angry. Another person in a wheelchair approached me and I thought, *Well, I guess I'll just pray for her anyway.* I prayed for the lady, and she jumped out of the wheelchair. Yes! Isn't God good? Inside I was so excited because I understood what God was teaching me—not everything happens immediately. We have to be patient and diligent and continue to do the work that God has called us to do. Do not let the enemy steal the person God has created you to be. Don't be discouraged. It is training—Kingdom training—for His army.

Fighting Back

For nine months I couldn't sleep. I had unexplained bruises and scratches all over my body. I didn't know what to do so I went to the church and said, "Can you please help me?" They thought I was crazy and said, "Put her in a mental institution." They didn't understand the warfare. For an entire weekend I stayed in my closet. After three days of being in a closet and crying to God, I came out of the closet. I had an experience with the Father like I had never had before and He healed me. In the Spirit I came out and started to talk to the Father. I stepped through a cloud and the Father started to download His Word to me. He was speaking to me through His Word. He said, "Daughter, if My Word abides in you, and you give My Word out, people will catch the vision, and they will be able to help set other people free." See, we don't have time for 50,000 hours of deliverance. The person who is going through deliverance is going through so much. We need to learn how to do deliverance right—people are depending on you. When I started stepping out, I was only saved a couple weeks—yet people were getting healed and delivered. We have to break through the past, to step into today, to step into the future. It's not about you; it's about the people around you who need help.

First, your heart better be right. There are times when demons do not want to come out and there are times when they leave and come back with their friends. The demon says, "I will return to the house I left." When it arrives, it finds the house unoccupied, swept clean, and put in order. Then it goes and takes with it seven other spirits more wicked than itself, and they go in and live there. And the final condition of that person is worse than the first. That is how it will be with this wicked generation (see Matt. 12:44-45).

New Beginnings

It is time for a new beginning. God is saying and asking us, "I'm getting ready to take some of you into a place you have never been before. You are going to come up against the wall; you are going to come up against the enemy giants. But what are you going to do?" See, it's all for one and one for all. We have to start having that mentality again. We love and prefer one another, even if we do not understand one another. That you would lay down your life.... God says in Galatians 5:9, "*A little yeast works through the whole batch of dough.*" A little yeast leavens everything. Likewise, our tongues can poison families, relationships, careers, and so on. We must speak life. We must lift each other up and support each other when the enemy giants are coming against us.

I returned home from a trip and became violently ill. I went to the doctor and was told that I had colon cancer. I told my doctor, "I'll be back in 22 days. I'll be back, and then you are going to take the blood test again." For 21 days, I was on my roof with my boots on and my swords in my hands, warring against satan and telling him that I would never die of cancer. And so for 21 days I prayed. I didn't tell anyone other than my sister-in-law because I was not speaking it out. So I was up on the roof with my sister-in-law, and we prayed for 21 days. On the twenty-second day, I went to the doctor and said, "You can take a blood test now, and I'll wait for the results." The doctor returned after a while and said, "Angela, the previous two tests confirmed that you have cancer. Now, this test shows that you have none!" Too many people accept things that are incorrect or untrue. We must accept new beginnings and declare that satan has no control over ourselves, our bodies, our families, or our ministries, and we must declare the promises of the Lord. We are on the road of life's journey. Bad things happen to good people too, but we don't have to accept it as status quo.

We are in the year 2011. The number 20 means redemption. And the number 11 means judgment. Break it down, and it means deliverance. Judgment is on the land right now. God needs us to redeem what He has given us, and that comes through the Word of God. And there are warriors in the Bible. We need strong warriors in the Body today.

Love One Another

There are 12 tribes in the Body of Christ, and we are supposed to embrace one another with beautiful nail-scared hands—not throw stones at each other. Judgment is so rampant worldwide these days, and yet the Father tells us in Matthew 7:1, *"Do not judge, or you too will be judged."* We may not understand what a person has gone through or what they have had to deal with, or where they are at in their walk with Christ, so it's easy to have misconceptions. Please do not judge the person, especially if you don't have his or her entire story.

Today, there are so many wounded warriors. They take criticism and judgments to heart. We need more people saying to the wounded, "Look, you can do this. You will not fail. If you listen and abide by the Word of God—you can make it!" Remember Proverbs 18:21 says *"death and life are in the power of the tongue"* and you must choose life (NKJV). People, we must encourage and speak life to our hurting brothers and sisters!

I was in Tennessee for a Baptist conference and there were about 700 people in attendance. A friend of mine who battled with cross-dressing came; he was a drag queen. He has since been saved and has remarried his wife! I asked him if he would come to the Baptist convention with me, and if he could bring some of his friends. Of course! So he brought seven drag queens all dressed in their garb. There were a few people who were gossiping and slandering these guys, and I said, "Where I come from, we have a song that goes, '1,2,3,4, all the religious spirits hit the door.' You know who you are, get out. And they left. All seven of these guys got saved, and one told me he was healed of AIDS through communion! What if we didn't let him in? We need to start inviting people who are in great darkness into our meetings. If we don't, how will they know the love of our Jesus? Just because someone doesn't look, smell, feel, act, dress, or sound like we do, doesn't mean God doesn't love that person and have great plans for them. Listen, when we step out, things shift. Once, I was able to preach for an hour in a drag bar and when I left, the owner gave me an open invitation to preach anytime I was back in the area; all because I stepped out to reach those in darkness.

If we pay attention in the spiritual realm and ask the Holy Spirit, "God, is there someone I can touch today?"—He will provide. Sometimes we walk by people and see no value in them. That breaks the Father's heart, because there is value in each one of us.

Your Living Inheritance

Take back what belongs to you. Enjoy a living inheritance; take what God is trying to give you—because you can. Nothing's going to stop you, but you. You are the only one who can stop you. They told me that I would never be anything. When I got saved, I had someone tell me I would never preach.

We need to hear about God and who He is; people need to be set free and understand who they are in Christ. Once we know who we are in Him, we will have all the authority and power to defeat all the challenges that face us.

Are you ready to step out into a bright and beautiful future?

• • •

Jesus, I thank You for being my healer and deliverer and for rescuing me out of darkness. Lord, I pray that You would reveal my living inheritance to me. Thank You for new beginnings and vision for the future. Holy Spirit, come invade my life and fill me with Your presence. God, teach me how to be more like You. Set me free from the things that have held me back. I invite You to take me deeper into Your presence and into deeper realms of intimacy with You. Lord, I want more of You. More love for others. More revelation and wisdom. More freedom and breakthrough. You are an amazing God, and I am thankful to serve You. In Jesus' name, amen.

Chapter 9

CRADLE TO COFFIN

by Robby Dawkins

I WAS BORN IN JAPAN. My parents were missionaries to Japan and before I was born, satan appeared to my mother and father, separately, and gave them this message: if you allow this baby to be born, we will kill both you (my mom) and the baby at birth. At that time in Japan, women could get an abortion. It was not legal in the United States, but it was in Japan. My mother's immediate thought was, *Obviously God has a purpose for this child, and I'm not going to put my hands on it, because God has him here for a purpose. I'm not going to go against God. I'm not going to fight God's purpose.* My mother had a spiritual depth in life that was incredible. I never heard her ever say anything bad about anybody.

So then satan appeared to my father in the same exact form. My parents never talked about it, though, until after my birth—my mother didn't want to worry my dad, and my dad didn't want to worry my mom. But they both prayed and they were interceding throughout the whole pregnancy.

I did not know this until many, many years later. My mother was very wise. She didn't tell me any of that stuff until I was into my 20s. When she shared that message with me, she said an angel appeared to her. The angel told her that because of her faithfulness I would be born on Easter Sunday morning, as a sign that God would fulfill His promise. This sealed His promise. Dad said that the doctor told him that my birth was like a warzone; my mother and father fought for my life. But everything turned out fine.

Now you would think after that sort of incredible entrance into the world that at two years of age I would levitate or something. No. And growing up in church, I really never saw a lot of incredible things happen. I never saw a lot of supernatural activity in my dad's church. We would see healings from time to time.

When I was about 9 years old, in the 1970s, my dad decided to start a home for runaway children and teenagers. So our home became a home for runaway teenagers, and the only available bed in our home was the one next to mine. If you are a parent, I don't recommend this by the way. But he brought in this young 16- or 17-year-old boy who was a heroin addict. My dad was helping him get off drugs, and I will never forget the experience.

It was about the third day into the process and it was messy— a lot of vomiting. It was really bad; the sickness that goes with detox was terrible. I didn't know if an alien or a demon or a legion of demons possessed the kid. It was very bizarre behavior. I remember waking up Saturday morning, and I saw him with his arm on the windowsill. His back was to me, and he was looking out the window. I said, "Hey, are you OK?" And

I'll never forget when he turned and looked at me with tears streaming down his face.

He said, "Robby, Jesus came in the room this morning and He took it all away. It's all gone. The addiction is gone. The past is gone. My shame is gone. I had been a male prostitute and... it's just all gone."

I jumped out of bed, ran to my parents' bedroom, and burst into the room. They jumped up and started questioning me, "What did he do to you? Are you OK?"

I told them what he said, and I burst into tears. Then I told my parents, "That's what I want to see the rest of my life."

Addicted to Seeing God Move

From that point on, I was addicted to seeing God move in that way and to seeing people change. I enjoyed hearing all of the teenagers' stories and seeing their transformations. We can so get caught up in the extreme power of things but it is really all about reaching into the garbage can of humanity, into broken, twisted, bent, and ruined lives, and seeing God transform them. Only He can set them on the right course, and only He has power to do that kind of work in them. Just like the woman at the well; it can be a life spring in you, and you can feed it to others. That's the Gospel; that's what God invites us to share.

I went through a rebellious time at 12 years of age. I know 12 isn't typically the real heinous, rebellious period, but for me it was. My rebellion did not come out in drugs, and I don't have any really cool, farfetched stories. But I remember sitting in the back pew of my dad's church and I would sneer at people as they walked by. I wanted them to leave. I wanted my dad's church to fail so we could go back to a normal life, which we never had because I grew up in ministry. I wanted something else. I started to hate church. I hated everything about it.

Then demonic spirits visited me in the night; it started very subtly. I would wake up the next day thinking, *Did that really happen?* It was sort of a twilight zone awake. The enemy wants us not to talk about it because that suppresses it and it keeps it undercover. To share it is to expose the enemy; we need to expose the enemy and be honest at every opportunity.

The church was located in a very poor urban area and on a regular basis drug addicts, gang bangers, and prostitutes would attend. I can tell you hours of unbelievable stories. We actually had a lesbian who led a stripper to the Lord. She was bringing her home to sleep with but didn't because she felt convicted, so she ended up bringing her to church the next day. Then she ended up going to a party and meeting a satanist, a guy who had 6-6-6 tattooed on his forehead. She gave him her number and said, "Call me sometime. I want to invite you to something." He thought that meant sex, so he was excited. One night she called him as she was heading to a home group meeting at church: "I know this may sound strange, but our church teaches that God speaks to us, and I kind of felt like God was speaking to me, telling me that I was supposed to come pick you up and take you to my home group." At that moment, the satanist dude was in such despair that he was standing on a ladder in his mother's basement with a rope around his neck about to jump off and kill himself when the phone rang.

And he said, "I'm a little tied up right now." Literally, those were his words. She said, "Well, I'm coming anyway." He thought, *Well, maybe this isn't too bad, I can have sex tonight before I kill myself. Then I'll come back and die.* She picked him up and in the group discussion we were talking about why we are here on the planet and why we were born. He decided to come to the meeting the next week, and the next week, and another week. We ended up baptizing him three months later along with five other people he brought to church. He totally stopped dealing drugs and all that. He started bringing people to church like crazy.

God does some really cool stuff.

But, let's get back to the story of me hating church. I remember my parents dragging me to a meeting. It was a powerful meeting of young people—2,000 teens worshiping God extravagantly. There was a woman minister there, and she stood up and gave the following prophecy. I'll never forget it as long as I live.

She said that there was a drummer in the audience and said, "I don't know where you are, and I don't know your name, but you're a drummer."

I was a drummer in my parents' church. I would drum and then go to the back pew and sneer. So I was sitting there and she continued, "This is what the Lord says to you." They were the words that Jesus said to Peter in Luke 22:31-32. "Simon, Simon, satan has the desire to sift you as wheat." Even before you were born, satan wanted to kill you because of what you'll do in the Kingdom. But the Lord Jesus Christ says to you today, 'But today I have prayed for you, and when you are completely turned around, strengthen your brother and that will be released to the nations.'"

Are You Calling Me?

It gripped me, and I felt electricity shoot through my body. I knew that God was speaking directly to me, and I mean it shook me. The next week I was in church and said, "Lord, are You really calling me to ministry? I have hated the ministry for the past several years. I've hated it." Those same demons have even visited my sons. I have six sons and the same demons have come and told my sons, "You will be one of us, and we will use you to advance our kingdom." These were the messages they spoke to me in the night and tormented me with.

While in church, I asked the Lord again, "Are You really calling me? Are You going to use me and do You want to use me to equip the Church, to minister the Gospel. Is that what You are really calling me to do...calling me to ministry?" And all of a sudden a woman stood up and gave a message in tongues for about a minute, which in tongues seems like an hour. When she stopped, my mother interpreted the tongues message and she said, "The Lord says 'yes' and that was it." The second after I prayed that prayer, He answered it. That's how quickly He responded. God prompted that woman to give the message, and then prompted Mom to tell me that the Lord said, "Yes." After that, I knew I had to be part of what God was doing and planned to do.

We started a Christian rock band. We were a horrible-sounding band, but we worshiped with all of our hearts; and this was before worship got really hip and cool. Nobody came to hear us, but we were not discouraged. We even made a light system out of paint cans. Most times we would set up on the front lawn of our home, and after the music, I would preach.

Fearless and Boldness

One Saturday night when I was 14, we set up in front of the church, and after we played some music, I started preaching. "Jesus wants to be in your life. He loves you, and today Jesus is calling you!" All of a sudden I felt the scaffolding of our stage shaking, and I saw this guy climbing up. I thought, *Maybe this is some dude bringing me some water or something.* I kept preaching. Then I heard him cussing and hollering profanity. I looked at our guitar player and his strap came undone and his guitar just dropped down off the stage and onto the ground. He looked scared for some reason.

The guy kept screaming and I felt him touching my head, but I didn't know why. Mom was at the light board and she started waving her arms frantically. I thought, *The Holy Spirit is hitting Mom right now. Look at the power this preaching has on her!* It turns out that the dude had a gun to my head. I didn't know it, so I just kept preaching. Everybody was in shock and a crowd started to gather.

Dad was our sound guy, and he wasn't sure what to do. Finally the pastor hollered, "All right, this is over, this stops now!" The guy was drunk and he climbed down and left. But he came back to church the next day and gave his life to Christ. He said to me, "I was shocked that a boy on the drums was so fearless. You just kept preaching without any fear whatsoever."

I was completely unaware of the gun to my head—I thought everyone was amazed at my powerful preaching. But the Lord spoke to me that day, "I want you to live as if you can't die. I want you to live every day the rest of your life knowing that all of your days are in My hands. I want you to live that way. I don't want you to live in fear. I don't want you to live in reaction. I want you to live as if every day is in My hands."

After that, I felt boldness in me, and I began to share more. A week or so later, this girl that I had been witnessing to on the playground came up to me and said, "Tell me that stuff again." I shared with her again; and right there in the sandbox, we knelt down and she gave her life to Christ. I believe my new boldness made the difference.

Many have incredible stories. Many think that God is just going to grab us and apprehend us and that giving a word from God to somebody is going to be God taking over our bodies or being filled and possessed with the Holy Spirit. But sometimes, it's just the simple act of telling someone about Jesus that makes all the difference in the world for that person.

Have you seen the movie *Men in Black*? Do you remember the bug? We think if God wants to give a word through us to somebody else that we are like the bug—the bug wasn't quite comfortable in the man's suit. He was an alien in a man's skin; and I think we sort of do that, too. We think that if God wants me to give a word to somebody that he's going to grab my body, and we need to say, "The Lord wants you to know I have a word for you. Jesus loves you and wants you to be just like me." Is that sort of what you think is going to happen? Do you think that if God wants you to do that then He will override your free will? No. He won't.

Desperate People

I was in my office one day, and I was really angry with my senior pastor. At that time, I was youth pastoring, and the pastor asked me to wash his car and to take his laundry to the cleaners. *I don't remember that being in my job description*, I thought, so I was upset. I hadn't been fasting, hadn't been praying, and I probably didn't even do my devotionals that day; but then the phone rang and a woman said, "I'm in a crisis!"

Now let me tell you something; crisis is always a friend of the Church. God loves desperate people; and when you put crisis and desperation together, you have the ingredients for a miracle. She said, "My father is going in for his third bypass surgery. The doctors don't think he's going to make it and there's nothing else they can do. We need somebody to help us. We're not church people. We're not even Christians." She continued, "We need somebody who can pray, burn a candle, do something...we just don't know what to do."

I thought, *OK, this lady is not even a Christian, but it doesn't matter. I'm going to go ahead and pray.* I said, "Let me pray for you. Father, I pray that You help this family in this time of loss. I pray that You would be with them. Dear God, please help them to have made some sort of arrangements, and I pray that You would be with them during this time, that You would comfort them in this time of loss, that You would just be with them and let them feel Your peace...."

I was saying this guy's eulogy before he's dead. I was digging a hole and pushing his body in and he was still alive. I didn't have any spiritual sense in me whatsoever. I wasn't feeling empowered. I wasn't feeling anointed. I hadn't done any fasting, nothing like that had prepared me. As I was praying, I remember the Lord speaking to me, "Get out on a limb." I thought, *What? Get out on a limb?*

First of all, I hate to be interrupted. It's rude. I was sitting there praying, and all of a sudden I was being interrupted by God. *Excuse me, I'm praying here.* This is one of the first times I remember God actually talking back to me while I was praying. But I thought at the time, *That's not Your job. My job is to talk and Yours is to listen, and basically You don't respond.*

He said, "Get out on a limb." *What limb? She's not even a Christian, like anything is going to happen. You know, surely this is going to happen with Christians but they're not even Christians. These are pagans.*

Then the Lord said, "Take a risk." *A risk, what risk?* None of what He was saying was sinking in. Then He said, "Open your mouth, and I will fill it."

Now I had heard that all my life, but I thought that applied to food. I thought God was saying that I was hungry, and He would give me food. *I'm not even hungry right now, why would I open my mouth.* I didn't understand. Then it occurred to me the Lord wanted me to take a risk. I said, "You know, ma'am, the Lord wants you to know that He's about to..." And I didn't know what I was going to say next, which is pretty much how I still do prophetic ministry today because I pick out people, and I have no clue what the Lord wants me to tell them until He speaks through me.

"...completely heal your father. And as a matter of fact, He's going to give him a brand-new heart, and He's going to give him brand-new lungs to go with it." She hadn't mentioned anything about lungs.

Have you ever said something and you wish you could catch the words before they reached someone's ears—bring them back and swallow them? And so all of a sudden, I said, "Now wait a minute. I have never prayed for anybody to be healed. You just need to be prepared." She said, "You said God is going to give my dad a new heart." I said, "Yes, but..." And she hung up the phone. Immediately, I felt prompted to prepare my resume. *I'm going to be fired, and that's if she doesn't sue the church.* This is bad, really bad. I was really sweating it.

Hours later, the woman called back. *Oh my God, I killed her dad. He's dead and it's my fault. I did it. He's dead. Why did I pray and say something about healing. What was I thinking?* I said, "Oh my gosh, I'm so sorry. I'm so sorry. I'm so, so sorry."

She said, "My dad is not dead; that's what I called to tell you. He's alive and when they opened his chest all of the previous scarring from the other surgeries was completely gone except on the outside and the pig valve was gone. The doctor said he has the heart of a 30-year-old man! I didn't even tell you that he had half of a lung removed on that side and now he has a whole lung!

I can't believe it, but I'm telling you that God healed my dad."

That next Sunday she brought copies of the medical documentation, the doctors' report. And that *next* Sunday, she, her husband, and her very young children, came to church, and they all gave their lives to Christ as well as her dad, mom, and brother.

All of that joy and healing and I wasn't even prepared or trained. I was just stepping out in faith, and I was completely blown away by God's faithfulness.

Miracles

I was invited to Princeton University to give three lectures about whether miracles happen today. Now let me just say, Princeton is a tough crowd. I remember thinking the whole time, *Lord, what are You going to do here?* God doesn't really show me a lot in advance. My 17-year-old son says doing this is like Christmas; you never know what's in the box. It could be an iPod or it could be air. You're not quite sure what you're going to get, but it's a blast expecting the unexpected.

So we were in one of the largest lecture halls at Princeton and I was teaching and answering a lot of hard questions—there were a lot of skeptics. I was not presenting at the seminary, by the way—this was at the main university, and the spiritual opposition was intense. Even the weather was intense. Fifteen minutes before the meeting started, a hailstorm came with lightning, which, they said, never happens at Princeton that time of year. And the hailstorm was mainly on campus, not in the surrounding community. It was really bizarre.

Toward the end of the meeting, as I was doing prophetic ministry, people started feeling slaps on their faces. Finger marks were visible, yet no one was actually slapping anyone. Demonic spirits were attacking people for being there. This was some of the biggest opposition I had ever encountered.

I asked the audience if anyone needed healing. "If you are in pain right now, come up." Fifteen came up, and 14 of the 15 were healed. The skeptics sat watching the incredible experience of healing. A picture of that was on the first page of the Princetonian the next day and the online article had more hits than any previous article, I was told. The group that invited me asked if I would consider going to Harvard and Yale. Absolutely! Now that's coming from a guy with a Bachelor's degree who was going up against PhDs, but I know that God will show up.

Three skeptics were standing over to the side, because I told the audience, "If you want to know if this is real, come up and stand to the side." We had just prayed, "Come, Holy Spirit," and I walked over to the outspoken skeptics. I said to them, "The Holy Spirit is coming on you right now." All of a sudden, the hands of two of the guys began to shake and their eyes opened widely, then their arms started to shake, and then their whole bodies shook. One of them dropped to the ground, his eyes were open, and he looked like a strip of bacon frying in a pan. The other guy began to feel intense heat all over his body. He was an atheist, and he said, "I believe in God. My mind has been changed." That's what we call the manifest presence of God!

It's You

These stories can sound so huge and exciting, but I believe that the next great move of God, the next great revival for your community or city, is sitting in your seat. You don't need somebody else to come in and do anything. It's you. You are the move of God. Satan is going to try to come and bring all sorts of obstacles in front of you. But you have to remember that when Jesus went into the wilderness to be tempted of the enemy, the Holy Spirit led him. I remember reading that and thinking, *Gee, that's just mean. The Holy Spirit was having a bad day and took Jesus with Him.*

But let me explain. Opposition is significant because we are developed and trained through it. When thoughts come—*I'm not good enough, I can't, I'm not able, I'm not that guy, I'm not that woman*—that's the enemy trying to minister unbelief to you. The unbelief that you will struggle with is not whether can God do it. The unbelief you will struggle with is whether God can do it through me. And my friend, you have to break through that struggle by doing it anyway.

You're not going to feel qualified and guess what—you're not. You're not going to feel capable and guess what—you're not. You're not going to feel good enough. You're going to feel disqualified. You're going to feel like a failure. Let me tell you something. I don't do it because I feel like a success. I do it because it pleases the Father; and the Father heart of God is in passionate pursuit of all of humanity. How do they know that He his passionately pursuing them? Because of me and my life and you and your life—that's the only way they'll know.

And so when we step into this ministry, we must know who we are in Christ. Let me tell you a different way to think about that. The enemy is going to fight you about knowing who you really are. The Bible says that they who know their God will be strong and do great exploits. Don't worry about who you are, worry about knowing who He is, and you will do great exploits. You will see your family, community, and city change and turn around.

Now back to Jesus being led *into* the wilderness by the Holy Spirit. When Jesus came *out* of the wilderness, the Holy Spirit was still leading Him, and He was full of the Holy Spirit and power. Most of our prayers are to avoid the opposition. I refer to these as boat prayers. Now let me ask you a question. If you were John on the Isle of Patmos, what would you be praying for? Why are you there? Why was John there? He was doing exactly what God wanted him to do. He was in obedience to God—living out his God-given destiny.

The Most Dangerous Place

Did anyone ever tell you that the safest place to be is in the center of God's will? That person lied to you. The *safest* place to be is not in the center of God's will; that is the most *dangerous* place to be—but it's the only way to live. You're going to be in danger. You're going to be in places where there are all sorts of opposition, where there are risks; and if you try to protect and guard yourself from it, you will never fulfill your potential. But if you are willing to lose your life for the sake of Jesus, for the sake of the Kingdom, for the purpose of God, you will have it and you will have more life than you can imagine.

Be willing to step out, because from the enemy's opposition, our faith will be solidified and we will be emboldened.

When John was on the Isle of Patmos, he probably didn't have day-to-day necessities like food and water or even protection from the sun, wind, or rain. If we were in that situation, what would be on our prayer list? A boat! *Get me off this rock!* That's what most of our prayers are tied up in. God, get me out of this circumstance, get me out of this hardship, get me out of this difficult job, and get me a new boss. You know I hate this job; fix my husband; change my wife; make my kids obey me— give me new kids, give mine to somebody else, I don't even like them anymore.

Most of our prayers are boat prayers: *God, get me out of this mess.* The disciples didn't pray those kinds of prayers. And Jesus' prayers were for perseverance. His were more like, "Lord, there are going to be hard things. Come to them; help them stay in unity; help them pursue love; help them stand firm and not compromise."

Why You, Not Me?

A woman wrote to me, "I've heard almost all of your stories about praying and having your prayers answered. I pray for stuff and nothing happens. Why you and not me?" I wrote and asked her to tell me the last five things she prayed for. She wrote, "My husband lost his job. I prayed he would get his job back and he didn't. We had debt as a result. I prayed the Lord would help us meet our bills. He didn't help us meet our bills. My daughter got sick. I prayed she would get better. She didn't get better. She got worse. You talked about praying for a car one time, for it to start, for people to believe in God. I prayed for our car because it broke down, and it wouldn't start. Then my mother-in-law got sick, and I prayed for her to be healed and she's still sick."

Do you see the problem? All of those prayers are about her. I wrote back, "Go find five people in your neighborhood who aren't Christians and pray for them just like you prayed for yourself. Write back and tell me that God does not hear you and answer your prayers." I never heard back from her. I am completely convinced it is because it happened—her prayers were answered.

The majority of people you and I pray for are in our Christian community. We pray for Christians. I could know 10 Christians who need healing and 10 people who are not Christians who need healing. Who do you think is going to be healed first? That's right, the non-Christians. I can pray for them and see it happen—boom!—instantly. But for the Christians, I have to pray three, five, 15 times. Why? I firmly believe there is greater opposition to them than to unbelievers. Satan thinks, *I've got them; I don't have to fight as hard.* I really believe that is the case. There's a war going on, but we spend all of our time in our own little world.

If you want to see more healing in Christians, you have to sow the seeds throughout unbelievers. We typically pray for the wrong crowd, in that we're only praying for Christians. We saw miraculous things at the Furious Love conference. God is in pursuit of His children. And do you know one of God's methods of pursuit? You and me. He pursues them using people like us.

Fully Transferable

We have to keep things in perspective and we have to believe that the ministry of Jesus is fully transferable. If you don't buy into the fact that the ministry of Jesus has been fully transferred to you, my friend, you're not going to see much happen.

We have a tendency to say, "But God, I don't have that ability." Your gift to God is *availability*, and He says, "You go first, and then My power will flow through you." That's how it works. Sometimes we would rather respond, "When you anoint me and electricity shoots from my fingertips, and powerful things happen, then I'll know that Your power is with me, and then I'll go." No. That's not how it works. God says, "You go, and I'll show up."

Be yourself. Don't try to pray like somebody else. Be yourself. God has called you to be you, and the ministry of Jesus is transferrable. Jesus said, I'm going away so the Holy Spirit will come on you to go do this stuff. When Jesus came, He didn't come as God and wearing His superhero powers. The Bible says that He denied His rights as God. He came as a human being, so from what power did He draw? The same power you and I draw from—the Holy Spirit. That was the source of His power. You have the same power source that Jesus had. He was fully human. He was fully man, filled with the Holy Spirit; thus, power came out because the Spirit was the source of His power. You need not wait for anything else—you have the power.

I know the truck driver who delivers stuff to our church. I always love talking to this guy and I always help unload the boxes. He says, "Robby, I'm just waiting on my healing ministry. God prophesied to me for years I was going to have a healing ministry." After hearing this often, I finally looked at him and said, "Hey, tell me, how many sick people have you prayed for?"

He said, "None. I haven't got my healing ministry yet." And I said, "Dude, you're not going to get your healing ministry until you start praying for sick people."

"Whoa, I know...but I have to wait on God."

"No. I think God is waiting on you."

God's idea of success is when we go. When we go to work for God, we will be successful. If we go to work for ourselves, we are going to be discouraged, disillusioned, frustrated, and irritated. When we work for God, we walk away knowing that something happens every time —even when it doesn't, even when it seems that it doesn't.

God wants to use us to see these things change. He wants to build in us, work in us, and He wants to give us understanding that we have His permission to step out and say things and do things that we would never do on our own. I don't believe that cancer is gone until I say it. I don't say that by saying the word of faith, but I believe in doing that I engage in power that God has sent here on earth. I put into action the change.

You are the missing ingredient for all of the people around you who need Christ in their lives. I don't say that to make you feel manipulated, to make you feel bad, or to make you feel like you have to do something. The Kingdom message is very simple. The Kingdom message is where the King is, and the King is there because you and I are there. Where the King is, Kingdom things happen, change happens.

When you and I show up, God has shown up. Christ in you is the hope of the world, and you are ambassadors of Jesus Christ. When we go out and share the Gospel, when we pray for the sick, we are stripping the kingdom of darkness of power and bringing it into the light and into the glory of God.

Remember, power comes for a purpose and its purpose is not our purpose—it's His purpose. Unfortunately, there are a lot of people trying to use power for their own purpose; and if we don't keep it focused on the King and bringing glory to the King, then nothing will happen. God calls us to the extreme, and we can't step out and play it safe.

I was in Sri Lanka several years ago with a friend of mine, DeSean. We were out in the middle of the jungle in a church. There were only about 25 people there, and I was praying and doing prophetic ministry. Then about 300 Buddhists showed up with machetes and torches, threatening to burn down the church and kill us.

I turned to DeSean and he interpreted what they were saying. "What do you want to do?" he asked me. My motto in such situations is to do whatever my host does. "DeSean, what do you think we should do?"

He said, "Well, if we go on preaching, it could get us killed."

I grabbed my Bible and said, "Brother, there's nothing in this Book that promised any of us we would get out of this life alive. I'm determined not to go quietly."

"Then we go on," he said, smiling.

Then a miracle happened. Within a few minutes all 300 Buddhists went away.

But after I left that day, they came back and nearly killed DeSean and the associate pastor. They split DeSean's face in half and nearly cut off his arm with their machetes. I sent an email to his wife, "Please tell me, is DeSean OK? Is he going to keep preaching in that area?" She went to the hospital and relayed the message of our prayers and covering and care for him. When she returned, she wrote, "Robby, DeSean told me to give you the message, 'We go on. We still go on.'"

My friend, you're going to face obstacles. You may be facing them right now. You're going to face discouragement, but we go on because God is worthy of us going on. It's not about us; it's about the glory of our King.

• • •

Father, I pray that this word will seep into our spirits, because, Lord, we don't feel qualified. We don't feel special enough to do Your work. We don't feel anointed. We don't feel like we have all that much; but, Lord, what we have we put into Your hands. We may not be sharp, we may not be slick; but, God, all You're asking is that we step out and share Your love with those around us. And in the name of Jesus, I pray that we realize that it isn't about a few select people—it's about the Body of Christ loving the world that is hurting, broken, rejected, wounded, and disconnected from the God who passionately loves them and wants to pursue them through us. May we hear that today. May that sink into our hearts. God, You're going to ask us to do things that are going to be dangerous, that are going to be scary—but may we always follow Your leading, even when it doesn't make sense, just because You say so. In Jesus' name, amen.

IN THE RIGHT HANDS, THIS BOOK WILL CHANGE LIVES!

Most of the people who need this message will not be looking for this book. To change their lives, you need to put a copy of this book in their hands.

> *But others (seeds) fell into good ground, and brought forth fruit, some a hundred-fold, some sixty-fold, some thirty-fold* (Matthew 13:8).

Our ministry is constantly seeking methods to find the good ground, the people who need this anointed message to change their lives. Will you help us reach these people?

> *Remember this—a farmer who plants only a few seeds will get a small crop. But the one who plants generously will get a generous crop* (2 Corinthians 9:6).

EXTEND THIS MINISTRY BY SOWING
3 BOOKS, 5 BOOKS, 10 BOOKS, OR MORE TODAY,
AND BECOME A LIFE CHANGER!

Thank you,

Don Nori Sr., Founder
Destiny Image
Since 1982

DESTINY IMAGE PUBLISHERS, INC.

"Promoting Inspired Lives."

VISIT OUR NEW SITE HOME AT
WWW.DESTINYIMAGE.COM

FREE SUBSCRIPTION TO DI NEWSLETTER

Receive free unpublished articles by top DI authors, exclusive
discounts, and free downloads from our best and newest books.
Visit www.destinyimage.com to subscribe.

Write to: Destiny Image
               P.O. Box 310
               Shippensburg, PA 17257-0310

Call: 1-800-722-6774

Email: orders@destinyimage.com

For a complete list of our titles or to place an order
online, visit www.destinyimage.com.